6/76

Cake Decorating and Sugarcraft

Evelyn Wallace

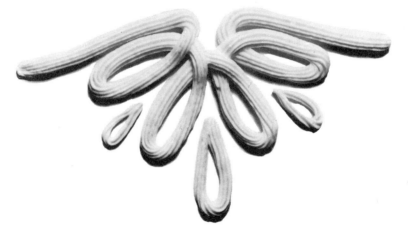

UPDATED EDITION

HAMLYN

LONDON · NEW YORK · SYDNEY · TORONTO

Contents

Acknowledgements

The author and publishers would like to thank the following for their help and co-operation:

The students and teachers at Woolwich Evening Institute, Eltham Institute, Plumstead Evening Institute and Thanet Adult Centre
Derek Davis and John Lee for their patience and help with the photography
The British Sugar Bureau
Syndication International

Illustrated by The Hayward Art Group (Elaine Handley)

Published by
The Hamlyn Publishing Group Limited
London · New York · Sydney · Toronto
Astronaut House, Feltham, Middlesex, England
© Copyright The Hamlyn Publishing Group Limited 1967
First published by George Newnes Limited 1967
Second edition 1969
Fifth impression 1972
Third edition 1975
Reprinted 1976
ISBN 0 600 31858 3
Printed Offset Litho in England by
Cox & Wyman Ltd, London, Fakenham and Reading

USEFUL FACTS AND FIGURES

NOTES ON METRICATION

In this book quantities have been given in both Imperial and metric measures. Exact conversion from Imperial to metric measures does not usually give very convenient working quantities, so for greater convenience the metric measures have been rounded off into units of 25 grammes. The following table shows the amounts to the nearest whole figure and the recommended equivalents.

Ounces/fluid ounces	Approx. g. and ml. to nearest whole figure	Recommended conversion to nearest unit of 25
1	28	25
2	57	50
3	85	75
4	113	100
5 ($\frac{1}{4}$ pint)	142	150
6	170	175
7	198	200
8	226	225
9	255	250
10 ($\frac{1}{2}$ pint)	283	275
16 (1 lb.)	456	450
20 (1 pint)	569	575

When converting quantities over 20 oz., first add the appropriate figures in the centre column, *then* adjust to the nearest unit of 25.

As a general guide, 1 kg. (1000 g.) equals 2.2 lb. or about 2 lb. 3 oz.; 1 litre (1000 ml.) equals 1.76 pints or almost $1\frac{3}{4}$ pints.

This method of conversion gives good results in nearly all recipes; however, in certain recipes a more accurate conversion is necessary to produce a balanced recipe.

Liquid measures The millilitre is a very small unit of measurement, so for ease, decilitres (units of 100 ml.) have been used in this book. In most cases it is perfectly satisfactory to round off the exact millilitre conversion to the nearest decilitre; thus $\frac{1}{4}$ pint (142 ml.) is $1\frac{1}{2}$ dl., $\frac{1}{2}$ pint (283 ml.) is 3 dl., $\frac{3}{4}$ pint (428 ml.) is 4 dl. and 1 pint (569 ml.) is 6 dl., or a generous $\frac{1}{2}$ litre. For quantities over 1 pint, litres and fractions of a litre have been given, using the conversion rate of $1\frac{3}{4}$ pints to 1 litre.

OVEN TEMPERATURE CHART

	°F	°C	Gas Mark
Very cool	225	110	$\frac{1}{4}$
	250	130	$\frac{1}{2}$
Cool	275	140	1
	300	150	2
Moderate	325	170	3
	350	180	4
Moderately hot	375	190	5
	400	200	6
Hot	425	220	7
	450	230	8
Very hot	475	240	9

As different makes of cookers vary and if you are in any doubt about the setting it is recommended that you refer to the manufacturer's temperature chart.

All spoon measures are level unless otherwise indicated.

Glucose syrup (liquid glucose) and gum tragacanth are obtainable from a chemist or pharmacy.

NOTES FOR AMERICAN USERS

Imperial	American
1 lb. butter	2 cups
1 lb. flour	4 cups
1 lb. granulated or castor sugar	2 cups
1 lb. icing or confectioners' sugar	$3\frac{1}{2}$ cups
1 lb. brown sugar	2 cups (firmly packed)
8 oz. stoned dates	$1\frac{1}{4}$ cups
1 lb. dried fruit	3 cups
4 oz. chopped nuts	1 cup
8 oz. glacé cherries	1 cup
4 oz. cocoa powder	1 cup
1 oz. flour	$\frac{1}{4}$ cup
1 oz. sugar	2 tablespoons
1 oz. butter	2 tablespoons

LIQUID MEASURES

$\frac{1}{4}$ pint liquid (milk, stock, water, etc.)	$\frac{2}{3}$ cup
$\frac{1}{2}$ pint liquid	$1\frac{1}{4}$ cups
1 pint liquid	$2\frac{1}{2}$ cups
2 pints liquid	5 cups

The Imperial pint is 20 fluid ounces whereas the American pint is 16 fluid ounces; the British standard tablespoon holds 17.7 millilitres whereas the American tablespoon holds 14.2 millilitres.

The following list gives American equivalents or substitutes for some terms, equipment and ingredients used in this book.

Imperial	American
Baking tin	Baking pan
Bicarbonate of soda	Baking soda
Biscuit mixture	Cookie dough
Cake board or drum	Cake circle
Cake mixture	Batter
Cocktail stick	Wooden toothpick
Cocoa powder	Unsweetened cocoa
Cornflour	Cornstarch
Deep cake tin	Spring form pan
Desiccated coconut	Shredded coconut
Double cream	Whipping/heavy cream
Fruit-flavoured jelly	Fruit-flavored jello
Greaseproof paper	Wax or parchment paper
Glacé cherries	Candied cherries
Grill	Broil/broiler
Icing bag	Pastry bag or decorating cone
Icing nail	Flower nail
Icing tube	Nozzle/tip
Kitchen paper	Paper towels
Mixer/liquidiser	Mixer/blender
Pastry cutters	Cookie cutters
Patty tins	Muffin pans/cups
Single cream	Coffee cream
Sultanas	Seedless white raisins
Swiss roll (tin)	Jelly roll (pan)
Treacle	Molasses
Unsalted butter	Sweet butter
Vanilla essence	Vanilla extract
Vanilla pod	Vanilla bean
Whisk	Whip/beat
White cooking fat	Shortening

Foreword

I have much pleasure in writing the foreword for the revised and updated edition of Cake Decorating and Sugarcraft by Evelyn Wallace. I have known Mrs. Wallace for a number of years and have been pleased to see the progress of her particular subject after she introduced classes in sugar decoration at this centre.

Mrs. Wallace is well qualified in her subject and has considerable experience which she is able to pass on to other teachers, and now to the ever growing number of readers to whom this book will appeal.

Mrs. Wallace tells me that she has had many letters of appreciation from readers, and this I can readily understand. Recently, she was invited by an American reader to visit America and take over classes to give some intensive teaching over a period of four months. This she did, travelling from classes in Canada to Texas and visiting San Francisco, Los Angeles, Washington and New York. During her extensive tour she visited shops and bakeries to gain more ideas on cake decorating and saw new equipment and materials, some of which she has introduced into Britain.

Whilst abroad, she was made the British representative of Cake Decorators International, a society that has a research department and which hopes to sponsor an annual convention, with a show and a competition, in a different area each year.

In extending her knowledge of this fascinating craft, Mrs. Wallace has visited most of the countries of Europe to obtain ideas, and she is hoping to visit Finland and Russia in the near future.

I would recommend her work to all those who take a special delight in the art of cake decorating and sugarcraft.

GEOFFREY C. SEDGWICK
Principal of Adult Education for Thanet
Kent Education Committee

Introduction

Everyone has some artistic ability and it is surprising how the simplest decoration on a cake can make it more interesting and appealing.

It is amazing what the amateur can achieve, so at the request of many friends and students, Cake Decorating and Sugarcraft has been revised and updated. Readers and students tell me that they have had much joy and spent many happy hours trying out the ideas and designs in the previous editions of the book. In this edition I have included some new ideas which you may like to try; after a little practice, they will become easier and more fascinating and bring fun and interest to the work done. More recipes have been added, but for new readers, the basic ones have been repeated.

Those students who now make a habit of looking in shop windows to gain ideas will be able to carry them out easily with the help given in this book. Indeed, ideas for cake icing designs will come to mind from looking at wallpaper, old plaster ceilings, carvings in wood, cathedrals, pieces of lace, embroidery and designs on Christmas and birthday cards.

When preparing to make a design for a cake for a special occasion, some theme should be chosen; for example, a few lines from a favourite piece of music can be chosen and these piped in icing as a centrepiece for the cake. A simple quotation is often a novelty. A few sugar flowers or a school crest will add extra interest; the picture on page 122, made for a 25th wedding anniversary, depicts the church in Greenwich where the wedding took place.

A decorated cake always makes an appreciated gift at Christmas or for a birthday and saves shopping for a gift with individuality.

An icing bag can produce its own minor masterpieces of craftsmanship which provide a means of self expression and satisfaction and give the same pleasure as floral art, embroidery, painting or the more usual pastime of knitting.

Welcome then to creative fun and all kinds of celebrations. This book will bring you happy times and fascinating moments in your cake decorating.

Evelyn Wallace.

Dedicated to Claire and Suzanne, who are always interested.

Icings, frostings and fillings

Shaking icing sugar through a doily or over strips of paper arranged in an open pattern.

Icing is a decorative covering for cakes and biscuits but certain forms of it can be used for modelling decorations. The most well known icings are those made from finely powdered or icing sugar mixed with either water or egg white to a thick pouring consistency, often with colouring and flavouring added. Other toppings and cake fillings can be made by blending icing sugar and butter to a creamy, spreading consistency while modelling icings use gelatine or glucose combined with icing or loaf sugar. There are many types suitable for different cakes and a variety of occasions. Other forms of cake covering such as almond paste – a blend of ground almonds and sugar – and pastillage (gum paste using royal icing strengthened with powdered tragacanth) are just some of the many techniques of cake decoration covered in this book.

Simple cake decorating ideas

To make a simple pattern with icing sugar, find a doily with a pretty, rather open pattern. Place this on a flat-topped cake and dredge icing sugar on to the cake through the spaces of the doily. Lift the doily carefully to reveal the pattern formed by the icing sugar.

Alternatively, arrange strips of paper on top of the cake in any design and dredge sugar over the cake in the same way. An unusual effect is obtained when the paper strips are lifted. By rubbing a drop or two of food colouring into the sugar with finger and thumb, shaded sugar can be made. When dry, dredge this coloured sugar over the cake. A fine sieve can be used in place of a dredger.

When thinking of decorating a cake, a number of foodstuffs such as cherries, angelica, nuts, chocolate buttons, orange and lemon sweets, sugar flowers, crystallised fruits and flowers come to mind. Any one of these can make an effective decoration with glacé icing, so before beginning to ice a cake, decide what effect it is wished to create. Consider the occasion and the type of cake before choosing the type of icing to be used. Advice is given at the beginning of the icing recipes on the most suitable type of cake to use for each icing.

Basic equipment for cake decoration

It is not necessary to have a wide selection of equipment to begin with. Most people will have what is required in the kitchen. The following is ample:

1-pint ($\frac{1}{2}$-litre) bowl	$\frac{1}{2}$-pint (3-dl.) measuring jug
1 teaspoon	greaseproof and waxed paper
1 flat wooden spoon, or spatula	scissors
nylon sieve	ruler

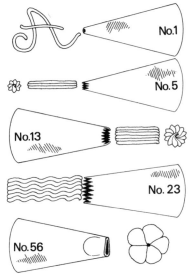

Icing tubes

Icing tubes can be bought as more experience is gained and more complicated designs are done. Only the five listed are really necessary to begin with.

small 8-point star tube (No. 5)
larger 12-point star tube (No. 13)
fine writing tube (No. 1)
ribbon tube with fluted edge (No. 23)
small petal tube (No. 56)

The numbers given refer to those used by Mathews. As different manufacturers use other numbers it is recommended that the manufacturers' lists are checked.

Icings

Glacé icing is an easy-to-make, everyday icing. It can be used on yeast buns, as a small centre on cup cakes, decorated with a cherry, or on Victoria sandwiches, sponge cakes, Madeira and light fruit cakes. It is not suitable for rich fruit cakes.

To make glacé icing for the top of a cake, use about 1 oz. (25 g.) icing sugar to 1 inch (2½ cm.) of cake: an 8-inch (20-cm.) cake takes about 8 oz. (225 g.) of icing sugar.

Put the sugar, unsifted, into a basin and add almost boiling water from the kettle. Stir with a wooden spoon until enough water has been added to make a creamy consistency thick enough to coat the back of the spoon with icing. Stir well until all the sugar is absorbed, but avoid beating, which causes air bubbles. If coloured icing is required, use a skewer dipped into a bottle of food colouring – never add colour to icing by pouring it straight from the bottle. Stir the icing well so that it is evenly mixed, but avoid taking too long or it will cool and not set well on the cake.

Stand the cake to be iced on a doily placed on a serving plate to avoid having to move the cake later and so cracking the icing.

Pour all the icing on to the cake, coaxing it across the top with a dry knife – a wet knife leaves pools of water.

Avoid pulling up the surface of the cake. Bring the icing just to the edge by turning the cake all the time. If the icing is too thin and runs down the sides, never try to scoop it up – this prevents setting. Leave the icing to dry and then cut off any surplus. With experience, icing can be mixed to just the right consistency to be coaxed to the edge of the cake and remain neat. Arrange any decoration required whilst the icing is soft.

Glacé icing

IMPERIAL/METRIC

8 oz./225 g. icing sugar
3 tablespoons hot water

Adding a drop of food colouring to icing from the end of a skewer.

To glacé ice the sides of a cake

The sides of the cake should be iced before the top, and coated with nuts or chocolate vermicelli – plain glacé icing does not usually look very attractive on the sides of a cake.

Rolling the iced sides of a cake in chopped nuts to coat them.

The easiest way to obtain a professional finish is to have ready some flaked or chopped and toasted almonds, chopped walnuts or toasted or coloured coconut on a sheet of greaseproof paper. To toast nuts, place them on an ovenproof plate under a hot grill or in a moderately hot oven, and allow to brown nicely, turning frequently with a spoon to prevent burning and to obtain an even colour. Coconut may be coloured by putting two or three drops of food colouring into a plateful of coconut and rubbing in the colour by hand until it is evenly mixed. For a less expensive decoration, use toasted oatmeal or crushed breakfast cereal, toasted cake or biscuit crumbs. Grated or curled chocolate or chocolate vermicelli may be used in place of the nuts.

Put 2–3 tablespoons icing sugar into a small basin and add a very little hot water to make the glacé icing. Spread the icing on the sides of the cake with a knife and roll the cake (holding it with both hands) in the nuts until the sides are evenly coated, pressing the nuts gently to the sides of the cake.

Jam or butter cream may be used in place of the glacé icing.

If a filling of jam or cream is to be used, always cut the cake after the sides have been coated and before the top is iced. If the cake is moved after glacé icing is put on the top surface, it will probably crack or wrinkle. Keeping a cake for a few days after icing can also cause wrinkling as the natural drying out process moves the icing.

If the cake has risen in the centre, turn it over and ice the bottom. The rounded cake top may well fit into a deep plate, but if not, a slice can always be cut off the top to make a good level surface – but to ice a cut surface successfully, it must first be brushed with apricot glaze to set the crumbs.

To make apricot glaze

With a teaspoon rub some apricot jam through a tea strainer or small sieve into a basin. Stand the basin in a pan of hot water, and when thoroughly hot, brush across the top of the cake and allow to set before icing. If the jam is very thick, stand the jar in hot water before sieving, or add a few drops of water to make the glaze spread easily. If the cake is to be kept a long time, boil the glaze after the water is added, otherwise it may go mouldy.

To glacé ice a cherry cake

Glacé ice the top of the cake over the set apricot glaze, and decorate with cherries, angelica, nuts or any other designs ingenuity suggests. Stems of angelica can be used with half cherries arranged as a branch in the cake centre, or as smaller bunches around the edge. The drawings opposite show ideas for decorations using cherries and angelica.

Flavoured, as well as coloured icing, can be made simply by adding a few drops of vanilla or almond essence, rose water,

Ideas for decorating the tops of cakes using angelica and cherries.

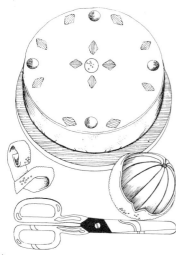

An orange cake decorated with pieces of orange rind, cut into shapes, and angelica.

orange flower water or peppermint essence, or orange or lemon juice, diluted to taste with very hot water. Icing sugar mixed with strong black coffee or strong cocoa produces good coffee and chocolate icing – add a small piece of butter to chocolate icing to give a shiny surface. Melted chocolate may also be used as an icing.

To glacé ice an orange or lemon cake

Using a potato peeler, peel the rind from an orange. Squeeze the juice from the orange, strain and heat gently in a saucepan. Mix icing sugar with the hot juice and carefully coat the top of the cake with the mixture. With scissors cut tiny rounds of peeled rind to look like little oranges and use these with pieces of angelica to decorate the cake. Strained lemon juice heated with hot water can also be used – decorate the cake with angelica and lemon shapes cut from the peel. Alternatively, tiny cocktail cutters can be used to make various shapes.

To glacé ice a domino cake

Make a cake in a 2-lb. (1-kg.) loaf tin using a Madeira mixture. If necessary, cut the top level and brush with apricot glaze. Spread the sides of the cake with a little glacé icing and coat with toasted nuts. Place the cake on a doily on a plate and pour white glacé icing on the top surface. Coax the icing just to the edge and allow to set.

Cut two strips of paper 2 inches (5 cm.) wide and the length of the width of the cake. Place the papers across the cake about $\frac{1}{8}$ inch ($\frac{1}{4}$ cm.) apart. Shave some chocolate finely with a knife and sprinkle between the inside edges of the paper. Press gently with the fingers – this makes the line on the top of the domino. Remove the paper and arrange chocolate buttons for the spots on the domino.

For small domino cakes, bake the mixture in a large flat tin. Ice all over the top with glacé icing and when set cut into strips about 3 inches ($7\frac{1}{2}$ cm.) wide. Make a line of chocolate as in the larger cake – or pipe a line of chocolate icing – down the centre of the length of each strip. Remove the paper and cut each strip across into fingers about 1 inch ($2\frac{1}{2}$ cm.) wide, wiping the knife before each new cake is cut. Use small pieces of chocolate or chocolate buttons for the domino numbers, or pipe the dots with chocolate icing. Place the individual cakes in paper cases to give an attractive finish.

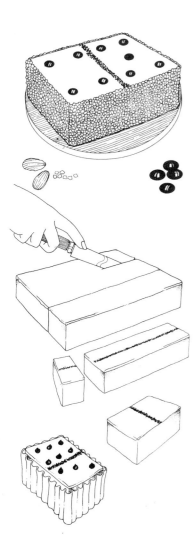

Domino cake. Cutting the large cake to make small domino cakes served in paper cases.

Fudge icing

IMPERIAL/METRIC

8 oz./225 g. icing sugar
1½ oz./40 g. margarine or butter
2 tablespoons milk or cream
pinch salt
3 drops vanilla essence, or 2
    teaspoons instant coffee or
    cocoa powder

Makes: sufficient to coat the top
and sides of a 7-inch (19-cm.)
cake. For a filling as well, double
the quantity.

This is a popular soft-textured icing generally used for less formal designs. It can be poured over a cake just before thickening, or with extra beating it can be made to take patterns using a knife or serrated scraper. It is an ideal icing as a filling, or for covering sandwich cakes, genoese sponges, Madeira and plain cakes, or very light fruit cakes. Again, this icing is not suitable for rich fruit cakes.

Sift the icing sugar into a bowl. Melt the butter or margarine slowly, but do not boil or allow to separate. Add the milk or cream and salt, and heat gently to 160°F. (71°C.), or just below simmering point. Keep at this temperature for 2 minutes and add the vanilla. Pour all at once over the sugar and beat until stiff. For coating the cake top and sides, pour over quickly just as the icing is beginning to stiffen – for making a pattern, beat the mixture a little longer. For coffee or chocolate fudge icing, pour the hot liquid very quickly over the instant coffee or cocoa powder and stir. Pour into the sugar all at once while still hot, and beat.

Mark the top with a knife, fork or serrated scraper in a pattern, as for butter cream (see page 20). Decorate with nuts etc.

Rich orange icing

IMPERIAL/METRIC

1 egg yolk
½ tablespoon orange juice
½ teaspoon lemon juice
8 oz./225 g. icing sugar

This icing is ideal for the top of cup cakes made in paper cases. It makes a good cake filling with the addition of a little more sugar and a knob of soft butter beaten well together.

Whisk together the egg yolk, orange and lemon juices and stir in the icing sugar to make a mixture with a spreading consistency. Coax this over the top of the cake (or cakes) until it is near the edges, but it should not be allowed to run down the sides. Place crystallised orange and lemon slices on the cake for decoration. Decorate small cakes with a circle of orange peel cut thinly from the surface of a fresh orange with a sharp knife or a potato peeler. A small piece of angelica can be used as a stem on the orange, and an oval piece for a leaf.

Creamy icing

IMPERIAL/METRIC

6 teaspoons hot milk (not boiled)
½ oz./15 g. butter, melted
6–8 oz./175–225 g. icing sugar
peppermint, almond or vanilla
    essence (optional)

Here is an icing which is suitable for a small child's cake.

Add the milk to the melted butter and heat until almost simmering, but do not allow to boil. Add to the unsifted icing sugar and mix to make a spreading consistency. Add the essence, if used. Whilst the icing is still hot, coat the top and sides of a 6-inch (15-cm.) Madeira cake. To decorate, use crystallised slices and coloured jelly sweets cut into pieces to form figures. Arrange these around the sides of the cake. Place a plastic knitting needle in the centre of the cake and tie coloured ribbons from the top of this to the sides so that the end of each ribbon is attached to a jelly figure, to represent a maypole.

Boiled fondant icing

Illustrated on page 91

IMPERIAL/METRIC

1 lb./450 g. loaf sugar
12 tablespoons water
1 tablespoon liquid glucose or
    pinch of cream of tartar

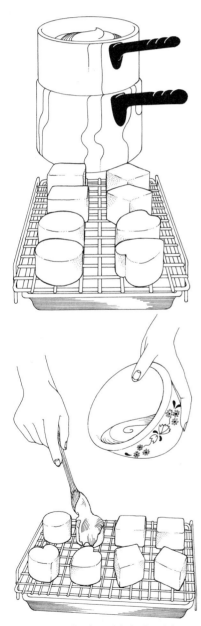

Covering small cakes with fondant icing.

Fondant icing has a delicious, mellow flavour, and keeps far better than glacé icing. It is used extensively by confectioners, but it can also be used by the housewife for coating small or large cakes, and sometimes as a base for royal icing. For good results, a sugar thermometer must be used. Have ready a cold, wet, marble slab, or if not possible, use a large, cold, wet, bowl.

Place the sugar and water in a saucepan and leave to stand while the sugar softens – overnight if possible. Place in a covered pan over a gentle heat to dissolve the sugar without stirring. Do not allow the sugar to boil. After 2 minutes remove the lid and add the glucose or a pinch of cream of tartar dissolved in 1 teaspoon of water. Put the sugar thermometer into the saucepan and when all the sugar is quite dissolved, bring to the boil slowly, brushing the sides of the pan with a brush dipped in cold water to prevent crystals forming. Boil steadily to 240°F. (115°C.), remove from the heat at once and allow the bubbles to subside. Pour the sugar mixture steadily in a thin stream on to the slab or into the bowl. Using a wooden or stainless steel spatula, work the fondant from the outside into the middle until white and firm. If the icing is in a bowl, leave it to cool a little before beating well. When the mixture begins to set, take up pieces and knead well until smooth. Put the pieces into a screw-top jar, screw down when cold and store until required.

To use the fondant
Have the cakes to be iced on a wire rack – small cakes should be brushed with hot apricot glaze (see page 8) or covered with a thin layer of almond paste. Large cakes need not be covered unless there are loose crumbs. Fondant icing is only suitable for the lighter cakes, such as Madeira or sponges, unless a covering of almond paste has been used first.

Make a *stock syrup* with 1 lb. (450 g.) sugar to ¾ pint (scant ½ litre) water. Heat together until all the sugar has dissolved, and then bring to the boil. Brush the sides of the pan with a brush dipped in cold water to prevent the sugar crystallising.

Put some of the fondant icing into a double saucepan and add a little of the stock syrup. When the mixture coats the back of the spoon and is 80–85°F. (27–30°C.) it is ready for use.

Pour the fondant icing steadily over the cakes and smooth as quickly as possible.

Fondant icing can also be used for simple piping on small or large cakes. The fondant in the jar keeps well and becomes more mellow with storing. Colourings and flavourings may always be added.

Ready-made fondant icing can be bought, but take care not to over-heat it when re-warming and thinning.

Any left-over stock syrup can be stored for future use, or used for making lemonade.

Modelling fondant

IMPERIAL/METRIC

2 teaspoons powdered gelatine
2 teaspoons hot water
¼ oz./15 g. white fat
8 oz./225 g. icing sugar, sifted
1 egg white
1 teaspoon lemon juice

This icing can be used as a covering for cakes in the same way as sugar paste, but it is specially useful for modelling flowers and animals or cutting into shapes for making sugar houses. For sugar boxes, to contain sweets, the edges may be joined together with royal icing. Colour may be added to this fondant.

Sprinkle the gelatine into the hot water, stir and stand, covered, to dissolve. Add the fat to melt it, then stir again. Sift the icing sugar into a bowl and make a well in the centre. Slightly whisk the egg white until it runs through the fork but is not stiff. Mix all the ingredients together to form a stiff paste. Roll out and use as required.

Caramel icing

IMPERIAL/METRIC

2 tablespoons castor sugar
3 oz./75 g. butter
5 tablespoons creamy milk
12 oz./350 g. icing sugar, sifted

Makes: sufficient to fill and cover a 7-inch (18-cm.) cake.

This is a richly-flavoured icing used effectively on the top and sides of a cake, or as a filling. It is most suitable for plain cakes such as sponges, Madeiras, or light sultana, cherry or walnut cakes.

Cut the cake through the centre, ready to put in a layer of the icing quickly. Heat the castor sugar gently in a small, heavy saucepan, until caramel is formed. Melt the butter in a second saucepan, but do not allow it to boil or separate. Add the milk to the butter and bring to 160°F. (71°C.), or just below simmering point. Pour this mixture into the caramel. Stir until all the caramel has dissolved. Pour over the icing sugar and beat until the icing is smooth and creamy and thick enough to spread. Sandwich together the two halves of the cake with some of the icing, and coat the top and sides.

Mark the top with a fork, knife, or serrated scraper, using any of the patterns given for butter cream (see page 20). Decorate with nuts etc.

Caramella icing

IMPERIAL/METRIC

¼ pint/1½ dl. water
10 oz./275 g. brown sugar
⅛ teaspoon cream of tartar
3-4 egg whites

Makes: sufficient to coat the top and sides of a 7-inch (18-cm.) cake.

Heat the water and sugar, stirring until the sugar has dissolved, then bring to the boil and cook, without stirring, until 270°F. (132°C.) is reached. (A little of the sugar mixture should form a brittle ball in a cup of cold water.) Brush the sides of the pan with a brush dipped in cold water to prevent crystals forming. Quickly stir in the cream of tartar dissolved in 2-3 drops of water. Pour over the beaten egg whites and continue to beat. When setting, pour over the cake and pull up in points with a knife.

Transparent icing

IMPERIAL/METRIC

8 oz./225 g. loaf or granulated
   sugar
¼ pint/1½ dl. water
1 teaspoon lemon juice

Dissolve the sugar and water together in a saucepan, then bring to the boil. Skim the mixture as it boils and brush the sides of the pan with a brush dipped in cold water to prevent crystals forming. Boil to 229°F. (109°C.) using a sugar thermometer. Cool slightly by dipping the bottom of the pan in cold water. Add the lemon juice and use to glaze almond boats, almond tart, Bakewell tart, Russian sandwich, almond petits fours, hot cross buns, rum babas etc.

Brittle icing

IMPERIAL/METRIC

1 lb./450 g. brown sugar
4 tablespoons water
½ oz./15 g. butter
2 teaspoons vinegar

Makes: sufficient to cover the top and sides of a 7-inch (18-cm.) cake.

In a heavy saucepan soak the sugar in the water for several hours, until dissolved. Add the butter and heat, without stirring, to boiling point. Continue boiling until a little of the mixture dropped in a cup of cold water forms a soft ball, then stir in the vinegar. Place the cake to be iced on a wire rack and pour the brittle icing over it evenly – do not try to spread this icing. Pour it from the pan as evenly and quickly as possible. The icing sets quickly and is a thin toffee-like coating which should crack when the cake is cut. Decorate with walnuts or Brazil nuts.

Gelatine icing

IMPERIAL/METRIC

½ oz./15 g. gelatine
¼ pint/1½ dl. water
1–2 lb./450–900 g. icing sugar
pinch citric acid or 1 teaspoon
   lemon juice

1 lb. (450 g.) sugar will cover a 7-inch (18-cm.) cake. Use more sugar to stiffen the icing for piping.

This is an economical icing and useful when eggs are expensive. It is light in texture and easy to use. It sets nicely on a flat-topped sponge or a cake covered previously with almond paste. If made stiff, it can be used for piping. It should be freshly made each time and a cake with gelatine icing should not be kept for long. Obviously it is not suitable for wedding cakes or special occasion cakes.

Mix the gelatine and water in a saucepan and heat gently, stirring all the time until the gelatine has dissolved. Make a well in the centre of 1 lb. (450 g.) icing sugar and into this gradually strain the gelatine liquid, beating it into the sugar until it is the stiffness required. Add the citric acid, and colour or flavour if wished. The icing should coat the back of the spoon for a covering icing, but for piping it should be made stiffer and beaten until it will hold up in points. This is a useful icing for birthday cakes when a quick result is required.

Real chocolate icing

IMPERIAL/METRIC

4 oz./100 g. plain chocolate
½ oz./15 g. butter

Makes: sufficient to cover the top of a 7-inch (18-cm.) cake.

Break up the chocolate into a basin and stand the basin in a pan of hot, not boiling, water. Cover to keep out the steam. Add the butter in small pieces. Beat well together when the chocolate is soft. Pour on to the top of a cake and decorate as required.

This icing may be spread on washed and dried beech leaves from the garden. Allow the icing to set in a cool place. When firm, peel the beech leaf away. The chocolate leaves make an attractive decoration on a cake.

This icing may be thinned with a little stock syrup (see page 11).

Magic chocolate icing

IMPERIAL/METRIC

2 oz./50 g. plain chocolate
1 small can sweetened condensed milk
2 teaspoons water

Makes: sufficient to coat the top and sides of an 8-inch (20-cm.) cake.

Melt the chocolate in a basin over a pan of hot water, or in the top of a double saucepan. Add the condensed milk, stir together over hot water for 5 minutes, or until thickened. Add the water and beat well. Spread over the top and sides of a sponge or sandwich cake.

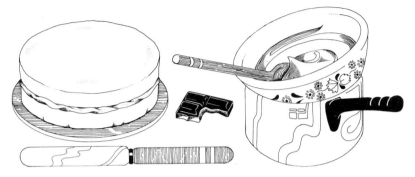

Frostings

This icing is crisp on the outside and soft inside. It can be used as a filling, as a soft smooth coating, or, with longer beating, as a rocky coating, although it is not hard like royal icing. A sugar thermometer is necessary for first-class results. This frosting is most suitable for the plainer type of cakes.

American frosting

IMPERIAL/METRIC

1 lb./450 g. loaf sugar
¼ pint/1½ dl. cold water
2 egg whites

American frosting is one of the more difficult icings to make. It requires practice to learn to know its appearance, and produce good results.

Place the sugar and water in a pan and leave to stand for a while. As this icing sets at once when it is made, have ready all the decorations and place the cake on an upturned plate or wire rack ready for icing. Place the pan over a gentle heat and make sure the sugar is completely dissolved before allowing it to boil. Bring the temperature up to 240°F. (115°C.). Meanwhile, using a hand whisk or an electric beater, beat the egg whites until very stiff. When the syrup has reached 240°F. (115°C.), allow the bubbles to subside and pour the syrup over the egg whites, *beating all the time*. Beat until the icing is very thick and fluffy and will pull up into peaks, and then spread quickly on to the cake. If wanted for a filling as well, have the cake separated into two or three layers and cover all the layers. Decorate the top quickly and place the layers together.

For a smoother surface, remove the beater from the icing a few minutes earlier, when the mixture will coat the back of a spoon. Place the cake on a wire rack, pour the frosting over it and leave to set – this icing will not be suitable for filling.

If liked, colouring may also be added.

To prevent graining – the sugar becoming hard or crystallising on the sides of the pan – a pastry brush dipped in cold water should be used to brush the sides of the pan as the sugar is boiling.

European frosting

IMPERIAL/METRIC

6 oz./175 g. unsweetened
   chocolate (or sweetened plain
   chocolate and less sugar)
1 lb./450 g. icing sugar
5 tablespoons hot water
6 egg yolks
3 oz./75 g. butter

Melt the chocolate in the top of a double saucepan; add the sugar and the water then remove from the heat and cool a little. Beat the egg yolks one at a time and add to the chocolate mixture stirring as each one is added. Melt the butter and add gradually. Replace the mixture over the hot water and heat until it is of a spreading consistency, taking care not to over-heat or the mixture may curdle. Use as a topping and filling for an 8-inch (20-cm.) sandwich cake. Decorate with wafer biscuits cut into shapes with scissors and arrange these in an upright position.

Syrup frosting

IMPERIAL/METRIC

2 egg whites
2 tablespoons golden syrup

This is a light, soft frosting which does not harden; it is used to decorate angel cakes.

Whisk the egg whites and syrup together in a bowl. Place the bowl over hot water and continue whisking until the mixture is sufficiently thick. Pour over the top of an 8-inch (20-cm.) angel cake. Decorate the top with crystallised fruits. Cake forks or a knife and fork will be required for eating this cake.

Mocha frosting

IMPERIAL/METRIC

12 oz./350 g. icing sugar
1½ oz./40 g. cocoa powder
5 tablespoons warm black coffee
2 oz./50 g. butter, melted
1 teaspoon vanilla essence

Sift the icing sugar and cocoa powder together twice. Add the warm black coffee and melted butter. Stir in the vanilla essence and pour, while warm, over the top and sides of an 8-inch (20-cm.) sandwich cake. Smooth evenly. This mixture may be used as a filling if a little more sugar is added. Decorate with blanched almonds.

Toppings and fillings

Chocolate crème au beurre

IMPERIAL/METRIC

4 oz./100 g. granulated or loaf
   sugar
4 tablespoons water
pinch cream of tartar
2 egg yolks
6 oz./175 g. butter or margarine
2½ oz./65 g. plain chocolate

Use this chocolate crème au beurre as a topping and filling for a 7-inch (18-cm.) plain or chocolate cake.

Place the sugar, water and cream of tartar in a small pan and dissolve the sugar slowly. Bring to the boil. When soft ball stage (236–240°F.; 113–115°C.) is reached, allow to cool then pour the sugar syrup slowly on to the beaten yolks whisking all the time. Cream the butter and gradually beat it into the syrup mixture. Lastly melt the chocolate in a basin over a pan of hot water then beat it into the mixture and use as required. If liked, decorate the top with toasted almonds.

Chocolate topping

IMPERIAL/METRIC

4 oz./100 g. plain chocolate
1 tablespoon rum
1 oz./25 g. icing sugar
½ pint/3 dl. double cream,
    whipped

Melt the chocolate in the top of a double saucepan over hot (not boiling) water. Cool then fold in the rum, icing sugar and whipped cream. Spread evenly and smoothly on the top of an 8-inch (20-cm.) sandwich cake. Decorate with small meringues (about 1 inch (2½ cm.) in diameter). Make some almond paste stems to use with the meringue tops. A little of the chocolate topping can be used to fix the stem to the mushroom top.

To form the word mushroom, use a stencil and shake icing sugar through the letters on to the chocolate topping.

Almond icing

IMPERIAL/METRIC

4 oz./100 g. castor sugar
4 oz./100 g. icing sugar
4 oz./100 g. ground almonds
1 egg

Makes: sufficient for an 8-inch (20-cm.) fruit cake.

Sift the sugars together and add the ground almonds. Mix with sufficient beaten egg to make a spreading consistency. Cover the top of the cake evenly, and smooth with a knife. Tie a piece of greaseproof paper around the cake and place the cake under the grill to brown the topping. Turn the cake round frequently to brown evenly. Care should be taken as this almond mixture will burn easily. Decorate the top with toasted whole almonds.

This topping may be used for a Simnel cake (see page 34).

Sherry topping

IMPERIAL/METRIC

1 egg white
¼ pint/1½ dl. double cream
1 oz./25 g. icing sugar
2 teaspoons sherry
decoration
2-oz./50-g. block plain
    chocolate
2-3 glacé cherries

Whisk the egg white and the cream separately and then combine them by folding lightly together. Fold in the sifted sugar and the sherry. Carefully spread over the top of a sandwich cake. Decorate with curls of chocolate scraped from the block of plain chocolate and the cherries cut into small pieces or halves. The drawing shows an arrangement with the chocolate and cherries.

The rich filling on page 25 may be used as a filling.

Making chocolate curls.
A sandwich cake decorated with chocolate curls and glacé cherries.

Butter cream or Vienna icing

IMPERIAL/METRIC

8 oz./225 g. unsalted butter
8 oz./225 g. icing sugar, sifted
colouring and flavouring
1 tablespoon evaporated milk
 (optional)

Makes: sufficient to cover an 8-inch (20-cm.) cake.

This is easy to make, ideal for a quick, simple cake, and can be used as a decoration or as a filling. It can be flavoured and coloured for use on Madeira cakes, sandwich cakes or sponges – it is not suitable for rich fruit cakes.

Cream together the butter and icing sugar. For a sweeter icing, use up to twice as much sugar as butter, but this is less good for piping. Any flavourings may be used – vanilla, almond essence, lemon or orange juice or squash, rose water, orange flower water, violet or peppermint flavourings, strong black coffee, instant coffee or cocoa powder. The colouring should match the flavouring: orange colour and orange flavouring, a pink colour and rose flavouring or green colouring and peppermint flavouring. A knife, fork or serrated scraper can be used to give an attractive finish.

Chocolate butter cream

IMPERIAL/METRIC

2 oz./50 g. icing sugar
2 teaspoons cocoa powder
2 oz./50 g. butter
few drops vanilla essence

Sift the sugar and cocoa powder. Add the butter and beat until smooth and creamy, then add the essence. Use for decorating a chocolate yule log at Christmas by spreading it over a chocolate Swiss roll and marking with a fork to represent the bark of a tree. Decorate with holly made from almond paste.

Continental butter cream

IMPERIAL/METRIC

7 oz./200 g. granulated sugar
4 tablespoons water
1 egg or 2 yolks
8 oz./225 g. butter or margarine
flavouring or liqueur

Warm the sugar in a saucepan gently without browning it, then add the water and allow the sugar to dissolve. Bring slowly to the boil, brushing the sides of the pan with a brush dipped in cold water to prevent crystals forming. When the mixture has reached 240°F. (115°C.), or forms a soft ball in a cup of cold water, remove from the heat and allow to cool a little. Beat the egg in a bowl and cream the butter in a second bowl. Dip the bottom of the saucepan in cold water for a second if insufficiently cooled, then slowly pour the sugar mixture into the egg in a thin stream, beating the egg all the time. (If too cold it will harden – if too hot it will curdle the egg.) Then gently beat this mixture into the creamed butter and add the flavouring.

Spread this cream over the top of an 8-inch (20-cm.) sponge cake and pull up, in points. Decorate with coloured sugar strands or chocolate vermicelli. This cream may also be used as a filling for a sandwich cake.

Valentine biscuits covered with glacé icing and decorated with royal icing (see page 100).

Two sandwich cakes covered with glacé icing. One is decorated with an eight-point star pattern using royal icing, the other with a sea scene (see page 66).

Butter cream designs

When making these designs, first spread a filling of butter cream and jam in the cake, and then spread the top of the cake with butter cream as evenly as possible with a palette knife. Avoid pulling up cake crumbs into the icing. It is a good plan to brush the top with apricot glaze (see page 8) first and allow to set.

1. Mark the cake top with lines as if cutting the cake in a diamond pattern. Keep wiping the knife free from butter cream.

2. Using the end of a small palette or dinner knife, draw the knife from side to side to give the swirled effect.

3. Use the flat side of the palette knife and pull up the butter cream in even points.

4. Make circular indentations all round the cake, then draw the point of the knife from the centre to the outside or from the outside to the centre, in eight positions. This fundamental method can be varied to make a variety of patterns.

To add a finishing touch, dredge the top lightly with fine icing sugar or sprinkle with chocolate vermicelli or coloured granulated sugar – sprinkle a few drops of food colouring on granulated sugar on a saucer and rub together with the fingers.

After decorating, put the cake in a cool place for the icing to harden. Butter cream has a high fat content and is liable to melt or become very soft if exposed to too great a heat.

Sandwich cakes topped with butter cream worked in various designs. The first three patterns are made with a small palette knife; the fourth pattern is worked with a scraper.

Chocolate log

Illustrated on page 22

IMPERIAL/METRIC

2–3 oz./50–75 g. margarine
2–3 oz./50–75 g. icing sugar, sifted
1–2 tablespoons cocoa powder
little vanilla essence
2 teaspoons evaporated milk (optional)
1 chocolate Swiss roll (bought or home-made)

Snow babies

Cream the margarine with the sifted icing sugar until very light. Add the sifted cocoa powder to make a dark colour, and flavour with vanilla essence. Beat in the evaporated milk, if used. Spread the cream thickly on the top and sides of the roll and mark with a fork to represent the bark of a tree. Decorate with sprigs of holly or ivy leaves made from almond paste and a model robin or woodpecker. If liked, sprinkle with icing sugar.

To make a log with a branch, cut a corner off the roll for one branch, or a corner from each end for two branches or knots. Place the cut side to the roll, joining and covering with a little butter cream so that the branch is at the correct angle from the roll. Mark the icing with a fork so that the bark on the branch is in keeping with the bark on the log.

To make an alpine roll, use a plain roll and white butter cream and follow the method given for the chocolate log. Smooth the cream with a knife and pull up in points to represent snow. Decorate with snow babies modelled from almond paste. Paint pink faces using food colouring and, using blue and red colouring, give the little figures eyes, shoes and rosebud mouths. Blue, red and green food colouring will give the dark colour if mixed in very small quantity. An artist's fine brush should be used for painting the faces.

Dougal cake

Illustrated on page 22

IMPERIAL/METRIC

4 oz./100 g. margarine
4 oz./100 g. icing sugar
1 Swiss roll (bought or
   home-made)
4 teaspoons cocoa powder
few drops vanilla essence

Cream the margarine with the sifted icing sugar. Spread a little of this white cream on the end of the Swiss roll for the face. Add the cocoa powder to the remaining butter cream and beat in the vanilla essence. When light and soft, spread over the sides of the Swiss roll. Mark with a fork, stroking the fork downwards to represent Dougal's hair. Pipe a little of the cream on to the face for eyes and a nose, or use liquorice sweets.

American butter cream

IMPERIAL/METRIC

1½ lb./¾ kg. icing sugar, sifted
small pinch salt
1 lb./450 g. white cooking fat
   or 4 oz./100 g. butter and
   12 oz./350 g. white cooking fat
few drops vanilla essence
1 egg white or little evaporated
   milk

Add half the sifted sugar and the salt to the white cooking fat and mix until smooth with a wooden spoon, or a mixer at slow speed. Add the flavouring and unbeaten egg white or evaporated milk; and the remaining sugar. Mix but do not over-beat. Store in a glass jar with screw top in a cool place, but not in the refrigerator. Use as a covering for cakes, or for piping or modelling. If the mixture is too soft for modelling, mix in a little cornflour or extra sifted sugar. If it is too stiff for piping, add a little more egg white or water. The butter cream should be smooth but not over-beaten.

Before using, always bring this butter cream to room temperature after storing in a cool place, and work it a little with a palette knife until smooth.

Chocolate mushrooms

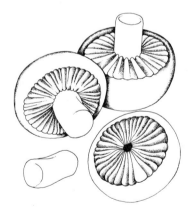

Make some chocolate buns using the chocolate cake recipe on page 179, but putting only a teaspoonful of the mixture in each tin. The buns should be flat on one side and rounded on the other. Make up some almond paste following the recipe on page 33 – about 2 oz. (50 g.) will cover 12 mushrooms. Roll out the almond paste thinly and cut into rounds with a biscuit cutter. Lightly coat the rounds of almond paste with apricot jam and press over the rounded side of the bun. This represents the top of the mushroom. Have ready some butter cream and add a little sifted cocoa powder to make the colour of the mushroom gills. Spread the butter cream thickly on to the flat side of the bun and mark lines with a fork from the centre outwards. Roll the remaining almond paste into a thin, round strip, and cut off the number of mushroom stalks needed. Press into the centre of each upturned mushroom.

Crème au beurre

IMPERIAL/METRIC

2 oz./50 g. castor sugar
¼ pint/1½ dl. milk
2 egg yolks, beaten
few drops vanilla essence
6 oz. /175 g. unsalted butter

Boil the sugar and milk, cool slightly and pour over the beaten eggs. Add the vanilla essence and cook in the top of a double saucepan until thickened. Cream the butter or margarine in a basin and whisk in the thickened egg mixture gradually.

Use some of this crème au beurre as a filling for a sponge cake and spread the remainder over the top. Decorate with strawberries or raspberries and pieces of angelica.

Snowman cake, chocolate log and Dougal cake (see pages 38, 20 and 21).

A cake coated with butter cream and decorated with butter cream roses.
A cake coated with coffee-flavoured butter cream and decorated with walnut
halves and glacé cherries. A serrated scraper has been used to make the pattern.

Marquetry in almond paste (see page 35). This may also be worked with
sugar paste.

Fillings

Top of the milk cream filling

IMPERIAL/METRIC

4 oz./100 g. butter or margarine
1 tablespoon castor sugar
2 tablespoons boiling water
2 tablespoons top of the milk

Cream the butter with the sugar and add the boiling water drop by drop, whisking all the time. Add very cold top of the milk, drop by drop. Leave in a cool place until firm.

This is a good filling for choux pastry buns, cream horns and sandwich cakes.

Rich cream filling

IMPERIAL/METRIC

1–2 egg yolks
1½ oz./40 g. icing sugar
½ pint/3 dl. double cream
few drops vanilla essence

Whisk the yolks and sugar together. Gently whip the cream in a second bowl, then fold into the yolk mixture. Add the vanilla essence and use as a filling for an 8-inch (20-cm.) sponge or sandwich cake.

Mock cream filling

IMPERIAL/METRIC

1½ teaspoons cornflour
¼ pint/1½ dl. milk
1–2 oz./25–50 g. butter
   (preferably unsalted) or
   margarine
1½ teaspoons castor sugar
few drops vanilla essence

Blend the cornflour and milk and cook, stirring, over a moderate heat until thickened and smooth. Leave to become quite cold. Cream the butter and sugar together, then gradually beat in the cold cornflour mixture. Add the vanilla essence.

Fresh cream filling

Fresh cream makes a very good filling but do not over-whip it or the cream will separate and form butter. When adding sugar or flavouring, stir it very gently into the lightly whipped cream. If the cream is required for piping, use a large nozzle or tube and a double greaseproof or nylon bag. Fresh fruit such as strawberries or raspberries, added to whipped cream makes a delicious filling.

24

Home-made cream filling (using a liquidiser)

IMPERIAL/METRIC

1 teaspoon gelatine
½ pint/3 dl. milk
8 oz./225 g. butter (preferably unsalted) or margarine
½ teaspoon castor sugar

Soak the gelatine in the milk in a small saucepan. Add the butter or margarine, cut into pieces, and the sugar. Heat very gently until the gelatine has dissolved and the butter melted, stirring all the time. (Do not allow the mixture to boil.) Cool to blood heat then pour into a liquidiser and blend at high speed for 1 minute. Pour into a jug and leave to cool for several hours.

Just before using, lightly whip the cream filling and use as a filling for a sponge or sandwich cake, a decoration on a trifle, or to serve with fruit. Use with chopped strawberries for a strawberry flan, or in place of the whipped cream in pavlova Sybil (see page 185), or to fill meringues.

Rich filling

IMPERIAL/METRIC

3 oz./75 g. butter or margarine
3 oz./75 g. icing sugar, sifted
1 egg yolk
1½ oz./40 g. cocoa powder, sifted (optional)
2–3 oz./50–75 g. ground almonds

Cream the butter and sugar together. Beat in the egg yolk and cocoa powder (if a dark filling is required). Mix in the ground almonds. Use to sandwich the two halves of a sandwich cake together.

This filling goes well with sherry topping (see page 16).

Confectioners' custard

IMPERIAL/METRIC

¾ oz./20 g. cornflour
½ pint/3 dl. milk
1 oz./25 g. castor sugar
1 teaspoon vanilla essence
2 egg yolks

Blend the cornflour with a little of the milk. Bring the remainder to the boil and pour on to the blended cornflour, stirring all the time. Return to the pan and cook for 2–3 minutes, stirring. Allow to cool slightly, then add the sugar, vanilla essence and egg yolks. Return to the heat and cook for 1–2 minutes, stirring. (Do not allow to boil.) Cover and leave to cool.

Use as a filling for cakes or choux pastry buns.

Nutty cream filling

IMPERIAL/METRIC

2 tablespoons water
1 small can condensed milk
8 oz./225 g. castor sugar
1 oz./25 g. drinking chocolate or ½ oz./15 g. cocoa powder
few drops vanilla essence
1 oz./25 g. nuts, chopped
4 oz./100 g. butter

Put the water, condensed milk, sugar and drinking chocolate or cocoa powder into a saucepan. Heat gently stirring all the time, then boil for 5 minutes. Leave to cool and stir in the vanilla essence, chopped nuts and creamed butter.

Use as a sandwich cake filling or as a filling between biscuits.

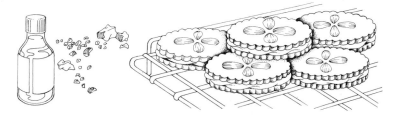

Animals modelled in almond paste (see page 43).

Two Swiss rolls covered and decorated with almond paste to represent Christmas crackers (see page 35).

A child's book cake. The edges are covered with royal icing; the cover may be made from almond or sugar paste (see page 37).

A cake in the form of a drum, covered with sugar paste (see page 38).

A birthday cake, for a 99-year-old, covered with white sugar paste and decorated with pink sugar paste roses. The edging is piped with royal icing.

Orange and lemon filling

IMPERIAL/METRIC

2 oz./50 g. cornflour
2 tablespoons lemon juice and
  juice of 2 oranges plus water to
  make up to ¾ pint/scant ½ litre
  liquid
3 oz./75 g. castor sugar
grated rind of 1 orange
1 oz./25 g. butter
2 egg yolks

Blend the cornflour with some of the liquid. Bring the remainder to the boil, then pour over the blended cornflour. Return to the pan and cook, stirring, until the mixture thickens and becomes clear. Add the sugar and orange rind. Cool slightly then beat in the butter and egg yolks.

Use as a filling for an 8-inch (20-cm.) sponge or plain cake.

Lady filling

IMPERIAL/METRIC

about 6 wafers
1 egg
1 egg yolk
4 oz./100 g. vanilla sugar
8 oz./225 g. castor sugar
3 oz./75 g. cocoa powder
  (optional)
3 oz./75 g. butter or margarine,
  melted
2 oz./50 g. hazelnuts, chopped
  and roasted
Victoria sandwich mixture baked
  in a 6-inch (15-cm.) square tin

Frosting small bunches of grapes and redcurrants.

Crumble the wafers coarsely. Beat the eggs and sugar until smooth and thick. Add the cocoa powder, if used, and mix well. Add the butter with the nuts and wafers. Put the mixture into a greased and paper-lined tin the same size as used for baking the Victoria sandwich. Smooth over evenly and place in the refrigerator for 2 hours. Cut the sandwich cake through the centre. When ready to serve, unmould the filling carefully and place between the two halves of the Victoria sandwich. Dredge the top with icing sugar through a doily.

Alternatively, a very attractive decoration to use is frosted grapes or redcurrants, when in season. To make these, choose sound grapes in small bunches or small bunches of redcurrants. Dip in beaten egg white and then coat with castor sugar; leave to dry on a plate. These should be prepared two to three days before using.

Keep this cake in the refrigerator until required.

Pineapple filling

IMPERIAL/METRIC

1 small can pineapple pieces or
  1 fresh pineapple
½ pint/3 dl. double cream
castor sugar to taste

Drain the canned pineapple, or peel and chop the fresh pineapple. Whip the cream. Fold the chopped pineapple into the cream and add a little sugar to taste.

(For economy, a not-too-stiff blancmange, made with water and pineapple juice, can be used in place of the cream.) Other fruits, such as canned peaches or apricots may be used as well as fresh fruits – raspberries and strawberries when in season. Glacé cherries add colour to the filling.

Apple filling

IMPERIAL/METRIC

2–3 cooking apples
2 oz./50 g. granulated sugar
2 tablespoons water
grated rind of 1 lemon
2–3 drops lemon juice
finely sieved cake crumbs (see method)
few drops food colouring

Peel the apples and cut into quarters. Dissolve the sugar in the water. Cool the syrup, put in the apple quarters, cover and stew gently until softened. Beat and drain off any liquid, then press through a nylon sieve. Add the lemon rind, juice, and enough sieved cake crumbs to give a firm mixture. Colour pale pink, green or yellow with a few drops of food colouring. Use as a filling for a sandwich cake. For decoration, make apples from almond paste and a stem from angelica. Paint one side of the apple rosy pink with food colouring and with brown food colouring paint in eyes and mouth to form a face. Dredge the top of the cake with icing sugar and decorate with the apple faces.

Jelly cream filling

IMPERIAL/METRIC

$\frac{1}{2}$ packet lemon jelly
$\frac{1}{4}$ pint/1$\frac{1}{2}$ dl. hot water
1 tablespoon cornflour
$\frac{1}{4}$ pint/1$\frac{1}{2}$ dl. milk
2 oz./50 g. granulated sugar
$\frac{1}{2}$ oz./15 g. butter or margarine
4 tablespoons cream
1 oz./25 g. glacé cherries, chopped

Dissolve the jelly in the hot water. Blend the cornflour and milk together. Bring to the boil, stirring and cook until thickened. Heat the sugar in a thick pan until it caramelises, but do not allow it to burn. Stir in the cornflour mixture and stir until the caramel has dissolved. Add the butter and stir until melted. Cool, then combine with the jelly, and fold in the cream and the chopped cherries. Have ready two layers of a baked Victoria sandwich cake. Rinse a cake tin the same size with cold water and pour in the jelly cream mixture. Spread smoothly on the top and place in the refrigerator to set for about 2 hours. When set, loosen the sides with a knife. Place one layer of the cake over the jelly cream and turn out. Place on a plate with a doily and place the second layer of cake over the set jelly cream. Decorate the top with icing sugar shaken through a doily, or glacé ice and decorate with cherries and angelica.

Lemon curd filling

IMPERIAL/METRIC

1 lb./450 g. granulated or loaf sugar
3 large lemons
8 oz./225 g. butter
3 whole eggs or 6 egg yolks

If loaf sugar is used, rub each lump of sugar very firmly over the lemons to extract the zest without taking the pith. If granulated sugar is used, grate the lemon rind using a fine grater, but avoid grating the white pith. Squeeze the juice from the lemons and strain it. Put the butter into the top of a double saucepan, or in a basin placed over a pan of hot water. When the butter has just melted, add the lemon juice, grated rind and sugar. Stir until the sugar has dissolved. In a second basin, beat the eggs very thoroughly. Pour the cooled lemon mixture over the beaten eggs, stirring. Return the mixture to the top of the double pan and heat to simmering point, stirring frequently until the curd is thick enough to coat the back of the spoon. Pour into small pots and cover tightly. Store in a cool place. Lemon curd will keep for about 6 weeks.

This curd can be used as a sandwich filling, or mixed with whipped cream and used as a cake filling.

A cake baked in a heart-shaped tin and covered with sugar paste to make a chocolate box. The cake tin is covered with sugar paste to represent the lid. It is decorated with royal icing piping and flowers.
A piped sugar royal icing basket filled with almond paste fruits, and a blue sugar pastillage plate decorated with white royal icing to resemble Wedgwood china.

Boxes of fruits made from almond paste (see page 41). These can be served as petits fours with the after-dinner coffee.

A cake decorated with royal icing fruit bowls filled with small fruits made from almond paste.

A 21st birthday cake decorated with a spray of roses made from almond paste.

A Christmas cake in the form of an open book. The cake is covered with sugar paste and decorated with Christmas figures modelled from sugar paste.

Nut filling

IMPERIAL/METRIC

3 tablespoons apricot jam
1 tablespoon chopped walnuts
3 tablespoons ground almonds
1 teaspoon vanilla essence

Rub the jam through a nylon sieve and stir in the remaining ingredients. Use as a filling in a 6- or 7-inch (15- or 18-cm.) sponge or sandwich cake and decorate the top with glacé icing and nuts.

Vanilla filling

IMPERIAL/METRIC

1 vanilla pod or 2-3 drops vanilla
    essence
$\frac{1}{2}$ pint/3 dl. milk
1 tablespoon cornflour
2 egg yolks
4 tablespoons double cream,
    whipped

Infuse the vanilla pod in the milk for about 1 hour, then bring the milk to boil and allow to cool. Remove the vanilla pod, wash in cold water, dry and store for future use. (If using vanilla essence stir it in with the cream.) Mix the cornflour with a little of the vanilla-flavoured milk. Add the rest of the milk. Bring to the boil, stirring all the time. Cook until thickened, stirring. Cool and beat in the egg yolks. Return to a low heat for about 1 minute to cook the egg – do not allow to boil. Cool, then fold in the whipped cream and vanilla essence, if used.

Pastry filling

IMPERIAL/METRIC

pastry
4 oz./100 g. plain flour
2 oz./50 g. butter
1 oz./25 g. castor sugar
1 egg yolk

7-8-inch/18-20-cm. baked sponge
    or sandwich cake
jam
whipped cream
decoration
cherries
angelica
nuts

Oven temperature: moderately hot (400°F., 200°C., Gas Mark 6)
Cooking time: about 15 minutes

To make the pastry, sieve the flour into a bowl. Rub in the butter, add the sugar and mix with the beaten egg yolk to form a dough. (All the yolk may not be required.) Roll out the pastry to $\frac{1}{4}$ inch ($\frac{1}{2}$ cm.) thick and cut out a round the same size as the sponge or sandwich cake. Bake this piece of pastry, preferably in the same tin used to bake the cake. Roll out the scraps of remaining pastry thinly and cut into $\frac{1}{4}$-inch ($\frac{1}{2}$-cm.) strips. Arrange these strips in S shapes or curls, making six or eight and place on a baking tray.

Bake with the pastry round in a moderately hot oven until lightly browned. Cool on a wire rack.

Cut the cake into two layers through the centre. Spread one half of the cake with jam and cream, place the baked pastry round on top and spread again with jam. Spread the second half of the cake with cream and place the cream side on top of the jam. Press gently together. Spread the top of the cake with cream and arrange the pastry curls as in the drawing. Arrange cherries and angelica between the curls and finish with nuts. If liked, the sides of the cake may be spread with jam and rolled in chopped nuts before the top is decorated.

This cake need not have a flat top. A well risen cake with a high centre gives the effect of a coronet with cherry and angelica jewels.

A sandwich cake filled with jam, cream and pastry filling and decorated with glacé cherries, angelica and pastry curls.

Technique of almond paste

Almond paste or almond icing, equally well known as marzipan, is most often used as a foundation for royal icing on wedding or birthday cakes, to prevent the rich cake from staining the white surface. But besides this practical function, almond paste can be used as a decoration in its own right, to make interesting and unusual designs in a variety of colours, and to mould flowers etc.

Almond paste or marzipan 1

IMPERIAL/METRIC

1 lb./450 g. castor sugar
1 lb./450 g. icing sugar
1 lb./450 g. ground almonds
1 tablespoon rum, brandy or whisky, or few drops lemon juice or orange flower water (optional)
2 large or 3 small eggs, or 4 egg yolks (the whites may be used for the royal icing)

Makes: sufficient for a thick covering on a 9-inch (23-cm.) cake.

Sift the two sugars into a bowl and add the ground almonds. Mix thoroughly. Make a well in the centre of the mixture, add the rum etc., if used. (If the cake is to be kept for some time the rum should be added.) Add the well beaten eggs gradually, stirring with a wooden spoon to form a stiff paste and adding only the necessary amount of liquid. If the paste is too soft it will be difficult to handle. Knead lightly until smooth, but avoid over-kneading as this may cause the almond paste to become greasy.

To cover a cake with almond paste

Dredge some cornflour on to a board and turn out all the paste. Form into a ball and divide in half. Using the hands, shape one half to fit the top of the cake, and roll out, using a little cornflour sprinkled on the rolling pin. If necessary, slice the top of the cake quite level, making sure that no crumbs become mixed in with the almond paste.

Brush the almond paste evenly almost to the edges with sieved apricot jam. Make sure that the round of almond paste is loose from the board. Place the cake, upside down, on the almond paste, press firmly and then carefully turn the whole thing over. In this way a flat top is assured.

If icing a round cake, divide the remaining piece of almond paste into two, and into four for a square cake. Roll into sausage shapes until each is long enough to encircle half the cake, or until each is the length of one side of a square cake. Use a piece of string to measure the round cake. Roll out the sausage shape to the right depth, measuring the depth of the cake with a knife, and spread the strips with sieved apricot jam. Place the cake on to the strips, using the same method as for the top. Roll a round cake along the strips, making a neat join. Work on the cake with the rolling pin to make a neat finish – the better the result of the almond paste, the easier it will be to obtain a good finish to the icing. Use a straight-sided jar rolled against the side of the cake for upright cake sides. Work similarly for a square cake.

Put the cake on to a deep silver board, cover with a tin and allow to dry for four or five days. Always allow the air to dry almond paste a little, otherwise the oil may come through and spoil the royal icing.

A larger amount of sugar is given in this recipe than some recipes call for, but the result is good and gives more almond paste, weight for weight, thus giving a better covering.

Covering the top and sides of a rich fruit cake with almond paste.

Almond paste 2

IMPERIAL/METRIC

1 lb./450 g. granulated or loaf sugar
$\frac{1}{4}$ pint/1$\frac{1}{2}$ dl. water
1 lb./450 g. ground almonds
1 egg
little almond essence or orange flower water

Makes: sufficient to cover a 9-inch (23-cm.) cake.

Put the sugar and water into a heavy-based pan and heat slowly until the sugar has dissolved. Bring to boil and cook until 240°F. (115°C.) is reached, or until the mixture forms a soft ball when tested in a cup of cold water. Remove from the heat, allow to cool slightly then stir in the almonds. Beat and stir in sufficient egg and almond essence or orange flower water to make a stiff paste. (If the cake is to be kept for some time add a little rum, whisky or brandy to the almond paste.)

Battenburg cake

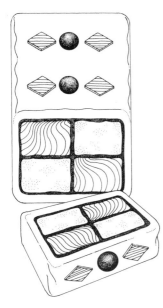

Prepare a Madeira cake or Victoria sandwich mixture, using two eggs etc. Have ready two greased and lined oblong, straight-sided tins, about 8 inches (20 cm.) by 3 inches (7$\frac{1}{2}$ cm.). Put half the mixture into one tin, and using food colouring, colour the rest of the mixture pink. Put the pink mixture into the second tin and bake as for a Victoria sandwich cake.

When cold, trim each cake in half, lengthwise, taking off a thin outer crust. Sandwich the four lengths together, using apricot jam, so that the pink is over the yellow and vice-versa, forming a square at each end, with four panes like a window. Press together.

Roll out 8 oz. (225 g.) almond paste to a neat square (large enough to completely enclose the cake) and spread with apricot jam. Place the prepared cake on the almond paste and fold the paste round the side of the cake. Make a neat join along one edge of the cake. Trim with a knife and define the edges of the finished cake with a fork or by pinching with the finger and thumb. Decorate with cherries and angelica.

The cake trimmings and any scraps of almond paste can be used to make a trifle with fruit juice, custard and cream.

Simnel cake

A Simnel cake topped with glacé icing and decorated with an Easter chicken and a sprig of palm.

Make up a rich fruit cake mixture and smooth half of it into the prepared tin.

Make up 8 oz. (225 g.) almond paste and cut into two pieces. Roll out one piece into a round the same size as the tin. Place this on the cake mixture in the tin. Place the remaining cake mixture on top. Hollow out the top of the cake mixture but avoid disturbing the almond paste. Bake in a moderate oven (325°F., 170°C., Gas Mark 3) for about 2$\frac{1}{2}$ hours, until the top is firm to the touch. Cool on a wire rack.

From the remaining piece of almond paste make a roll long enough to encircle the top edge of the cake. Brush the cake edge with jam and fit on the roll of almond paste, pressing it firmly and neatly. Prick the top edge with a fork and brush with beaten egg. Tie greased paper around the edge of the cake, protecting the centre with a piece of foil, and place it in a hot oven (425°F.,

A Mothers' Day cake topped with glacé icing and decorated with piped violets.

220°C., Gas Mark 7) or under the grill, turning frequently until the almond paste is evenly browned.

When the cake is quite cold, fill the centre of the ring of almond paste with glacé icing or thin royal icing. Arrange piped flowers in a spray in the centre, or decorate the top with an almond paste bird's nest (see page 42), or cherries and angelica. Large round balls of almond paste are often placed around the edge of the cake in place of the roll, but make sure the balls touch each other, otherwise the icing will run out between them, and down the sides of the cake.

If the cake is to be kept for a long time, a thin layer of almond paste put under the icing gives a better foundation. Allow the almond paste to dry a little before pouring in the icing. Finally, arrange a paper frill around the sides of the cake.

This cake is also known as a Mothers' Day cake.

Cracker cake

Illustrated on page 26

IMPERIAL/METRIC

red food colouring
8 oz./225 g. almond paste or
    modelling fondant
apricot jam
jam-filled Swiss roll (bought or
    home-made)

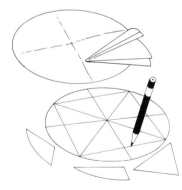

Preparing the paper pattern for a marquetry design.

Work a few drops of food colouring into the almond paste or modelling fondant to make it an even colour throughout. Roll out the almond paste to an oblong, using a little cornflour on the board, large enough to completely enclose the Swiss roll. Brush the oblong with apricot jam, leaving a clear margin around the edge. Wrap the Swiss roll in the almond paste, making the join underneath and as neat as possible. With scissors, snip the ends neatly. Decorate with almond paste flowers or pictures and tie with braid or ribbon, or with almond paste coloured a contrasting colour.

Marquetry with almond paste *Illustrated on page 23*
Experiment with the fascinating patterns that can be made using almond paste as a cake decoration; it is most suitable on a sponge or light fruit cake. Cut a circle or square of paper to fit the top of the cake, fold the paper in half, in half again, and in half again, so that when opened out, there are eight folded sections (see drawing opposite). Now divide these sections by drawing lines through each one, to form a geometrical pattern (see drawing opposite). Many other designs are possible.

Now decide on the way in which colour will give most effect to the pattern. Trace the pattern on to a piece of tracing or grease-proof paper, and cut out each section, numbering according to the planned colour, number all green sections 1, all pink, 2, etc.

Colour some of the almond paste pink, and roll out to $\frac{1}{4}$ inch ($\frac{1}{2}$ cm.) thick, using a little cornflour on the board. Using the sections of paper numbered 2, cut out corresponding shapes of the pink almond paste and place them on the original pattern. Continue with the green paste in the same way, until all the sections are completed.

Coat the sides of the cake with jam, and roll in desiccated

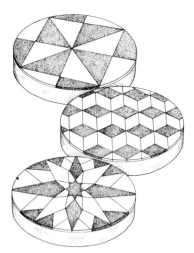

Marquetry designs worked in coloured almond paste.

coconut or toasted nuts. Fill in any cracks on the top of the cake with almond paste, making a good surface as the almond paste will take the shape of the cake. Spread with jam, lift the pattern pieces carefully from the paper, and place one by one in position on the cake. Take care not to stretch the almond paste or spoil the shape in any way. When the pattern is completed, gently rub the surface with the hand to neaten the joins.

For special occasions, scenes can be cut out illustrating special events and objects. Children's books and old needlework books usually produce an endless fund of good pattern ideas.

It is possible to do this marquetry with sugar paste, but it is more liable to stretch out of shape; much more care is needed when placing the pieces on the cake, and it is advisable to attempt less elaborate designs with the sugar paste.

Sugar paste or cold fondant

IMPERIAL/METRIC

1 lb./450 g. icing sugar
1–2 oz./25–50 g. liquid glucose
1 egg white
2–4 teaspoons lemon juice or
  vanilla essence
1 teaspoon glycerine (optional)

Makes: sufficient to cover an 8-inch (20-cm.) cake.

Children are not always fond of almond paste; this sugar paste makes a very good substitute covering for all cakes, especially ones for children's parties when discarded almond paste is often left on the sides of the plates!

Sift the icing sugar into a basin. If the glucose is stiff, stand the jar in a saucepan of hot water for a few minutes. Make a well in the centre of the sugar and add the glucose, whisked egg white, flavouring and glycerine, if used. Mix thoroughly, dust the hands with a little cornflour, and knead the mixture well, adding more sugar as required, to make a stiff paste – the amount of sugar needed will depend on the size of the egg white used. Plenty of kneading will be required before the mixture has a smooth, fine texture.

Dredge the board with cornflour, and roll out the sugar paste. Follow the directions given on page 33 for putting almond paste on a cake, but make sure the surface is quite flat, as any unevenness will show through the sugar paste. With a little cornflour on the fingers, rub the top of the sugar paste to give a smooth, shiny, polished finish. After drying for a little while, the cake may be coated with royal icing, or decorated with piping straight on to the shiny surface of the sugar paste.

It is possible to put a layer of almond paste before a top icing of sugar paste. The result is good, and the taste of the sugar paste is improved. This method is not suitable for icing a wedding cake with pillars, but many people prefer it to royal icing for Christmas and birthday cakes.

Experiment by indenting the smooth surface of the sugar paste with a serrated scraper, and decorating the top and sides with flowers moulded from sugar paste coloured with a few drops of food colouring. If sugar paste is to be used for flowers it is essential not to add glycerine as this would make it too soft for modelling.

Roses modelled in sugar paste.

36

Book cake

Illustrated on page 26

IMPERIAL/METRIC

piece of plain cake about 6 inches
    (15 cm.) by 8 inches (20 cm.)
    by 2 inches (5 cm.)
8 oz./225 g. almond paste or
    sugar paste
about 4 tablespoons royal icing
apricot jam

Trim the cake neatly and cover three sides (the top, bottom and right-hand side) with a very thin layer of almond paste – brush the almond paste with apricot jam to ensure it sticks to the cake. Coat the three almond-covered sides with royal icing and scrape with a fork to represent pages. Leave to dry overnight.

Reserve a small piece of almond paste for making decorative figures and colour the rest pink or any other colour. Roll out the pink almond paste, cut two pieces for the back and front covers of the book and make a strip for the back binding. Coat the back cover piece of paste with jam and place the cake in position on it. Brush the top cover of paste with apricot jam and place on the cake. Roll lightly with a rolling pin to obtain a good shape. Put a little jam on the edge for the back binding and arrange in position. Next, colour the remaining paste as required and use for a descriptive picture. One way to obtain these figures is to trace a suitable picture from a child's book and cut the tracing in pieces. Use these pieces as a pattern to cut up the almond paste. Stick them in position with jam. Roll lightly or press in place. Finally, pipe the title of the book with royal icing.

Santa Claus cake

IMPERIAL/METRIC

1 jam-filled Swiss roll (bought or
    home-made)
about 2 tablespoons royal icing
8 oz./225 g. sugar paste
red, blue and brown food
    colouring

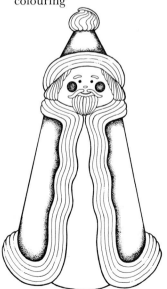

Making a cloak for Santa Claus from almond paste.

Stand the Swiss roll, on one end, on a cake board and secure it to the board with a little royal icing. Also insert a fine knitting needle or skewer through the length of the Swiss roll to the board.

Take a small piece of the sugar paste and model it into a round shape to represent Santa's head and place on top of the Swiss roll securing it with a little royal icing. Colour the remaining sugar paste with red food colouring and roll it out fairly thinly on a board dusted with cornflour. Make two paper pattern triangles (one to form a pointed cap and a larger one to make a cloak). Using these patterns as a guide, cut two triangles from the rolled out sugar paste. Cut off the top point of the larger triangle as shown in the drawing. Arrange the smaller triangle on Santa's head and wrap the larger one around the Swiss roll as a cloak. Leave aside for the sugar paste to dry.

Fill a paper icing bag with the remaining royal icing, cut a small piece from the bottom and pipe around the top, bottom and sides of the cloak to represent fur. Also pipe around the edge of the cap. Pipe whiskers on Santa's chin and pipe in hair and eyebrows. Using an artist's brush and food colouring, paint in a face with rosy cheeks. Using blue or brown food colouring, paint in the eyes.

Child's drum cake

Illustrated on page 26

IMPERIAL/METRIC

Madeira cake mixture (see page
  179)
1 lb./450 g. sugar paste
jam
few drops red food colouring
2 tablespoons royal icing

Use double quantity Madeira
cake mixture and bake it in a
deep, round 6-inch (15-cm.) cake
tin.

Cut a slice from the top of the cake to make the top quite flat. Roll out two-thirds of the sugar paste on a board sprinkled with cornflour to make a strip, the depth of the cake, and long enough to go all around. Brush the paste with a thin layer of jam. Roll the cake along the strip of paste allowing the cake to pick up the paste. Press the join with the fingertips to give a neat finish. Roll out most of the remaining paste and cut a circle for the top. Brush with jam and place on the top of the cake. Rub the surface gently with a little cornflour to make it smooth and shiny. Press the edges together to give a neat finish. Work a few drops of red food colouring into some of the remaining paste and roll it out into two strips and place one around the top edge of the cake and one around the base of the cake. Mould two drumsticks from the remaining white paste. Pipe on the decorations, with the royal icing, as shown in the picture.

Snowman cake

Illustrated on page 22

IMPERIAL/METRIC

2 Swiss rolls, or fruit cake
  mixture baked in a loaf tin
1 lb./450 g. sugar paste

From one of the Swiss rolls cut off a piece large enough to represent the head (or cut a piece from the fruit cake). Trim the piece roughly to a round. Roll out the sugar paste on a board lightly sprinkled with cornflour. Wrap it around the second Swiss roll (or the piece of fruit cake) and the piece shaped for the head to completely enclose it. Rub the paste with the fingertips dipped in a little cornflour to give a shiny surface and to remove the cracks and joins. Stand the roll on a cake board and place the head on top. Insert a long thin knitting needle through the centre to support the snowman. Tie a ribbon round the neck (or make one from scraps of sugar paste) and make a cap from sugar paste as shown in the picture. If liked the cap may be decorated with lines of coloured icing. Make a face and buttons from left-over pieces of sugar paste. Paint in any detail with food colouring and a fine brush. If liked the board may be spread with royal icing, roughed up to look like snow, and sprinkled with granulated sugar.

To model cake decorations

Modelling fruit, flowers, small figures and animals is really an art, but with experience, and by carefully following a few instructions, most people can produce good results.

Before actually beginning to model, try to find a specimen flower or fruit to copy, or even a picture, as guidance. Almond paste, modelling fondant, pastillage and sugar paste are ideal icings for modelling. If using almond paste use the following proportions:

4 oz./100 g. finely ground almonds
8 oz./200 g. icing sugar, sifted
1 egg white

Roses *Illustrated on page 62*

These are one of the most popular cake decorations and very easily modelled. Either bought or home-made almond paste may be used. If making your own almond paste for modelling use all icing sugar and egg white (as above) to mix the paste. Soya flour is sometimes used in a modelling paste, mixed with an equal quantity of icing sugar and egg white. Sugar paste models well, but the flowers must be kept in a dry place, as they can easily lose their shape and become sticky. Pay special attention to hygiene and always wash the hands before beginning to model.

Roll out the paste on a practice board (see page 53), or a wooden board, lightly dredged with cornflour. For a basket of roses, one or two natural-coloured paste flowers can be made first, and then mixed with deeper coloured roses.

Take a piece of the paste to be coloured and press a hollow in the centre. Add a few drops of food colouring, or a little powdered colour, and work gently until fairly evenly mixed. At first keep the colouring quite pale and, after making a few flowers, add more colour for darker roses. Avoid over-kneading, as this makes the almond paste oily, although a little royal icing or egg white and icing sugar can occasionally bring back the paste to the right consistency. Always keep the paste covered when not in use.

For the basic shape of the rose, make a solid cone of paste, about ½ inch (1 cm.) high and ½ inch (1 cm.) across the base. Roll out the remaining paste on a board sprinkled with cornflour to about ⅛ inch (¼ cm.) thick and, using a small round cocktail cutter, cut a small circle about the size of a new penny. The size of the cutter and thickness of the paste will determine the size of the rose petal. Do not cut more than two or three circles at a time, as the edges dry and will make cracked petals. Cover the paste on the board with a slightly damp cloth while moulding the petals.

Hold the edge of one of the small circles in the left hand, dust the fingers of the other hand with a very little cornflour, and proceed to press the rest of the circle of paste until it is as thin as paper. Held up to the light it should be possible to see daylight through it. The piece of the circle between the left thumb and finger should

Making roses for decoration from almond paste.

be kept thick, as this helps to build up the centre of the rose. Wrap this thin petal around the cone, completely enclosing it. The base of the petal – that is, the thick part – should be dampened with a little egg white or water, using a small paint brush.

Thin out a second petal, keeping the thick base in the left thumb and finger, and dipping the right thumb and finger in a little cornflour. Moisten the base and place this petal behind the first closed one, curling it back slightly. The rose heart must never protrude above the petal.

Continue making petals and placing in position, curling each one back a little more. Three petals are usually sufficient to encircle the first closed one. For a small rose, four petals in all are enough, but individual judgment should be relied upon to continue adding petals until the rose looks finished. To curve the outer petals, shape the circle of paste in the hollow of the hand, or over a hard-boiled egg.

To make a shaded rose, press together a circle of yellow paste, and a circle of pink. Cut to the right size, and continue pressing to complete the petal. Again, this is an art, and requires a little practice and patience in order to know how to place the petals for the best effect. Avoid pressing the rose centre into a long shape or it may lose its form and begin to resemble a cabbage. Also avoid putting too many petals on a rose. To make a bigger rose it is better to use a larger circle of paste than extra petals. If the base of the rose does become long, cut off a little with a knife or scissors before leaving it to dry. Any left-over paste should be wrapped in waxed paper and stored in a screw-top jar – even small pieces come in useful for modelling.

Have an egg box ready for the completed flowers, each part lined with a little greaseproof or waxed paper. Place the roses separately in each compartment to keep them from breaking.

To give a realistic finish to a rose, dust it with a little carmine powder – use this only with almond paste roses. Insert a piece of rustless wire in the base of the rose by heating the wire until very hot and then pushing it in position. This melts the sugar, which soon cools again and sets, fastening the rose to the wire. Place in a dry room for a while to harden the rose, then hold it over a pan of boiling water to coat with steam. Have ready some carmine powder on greaseproof paper. Hold the steamed rose over the paper and dust the powder on to the petals, using a fine brush. Shake gently to remove surplus, and return any dry powder to the bottle. Cover the wire with green paste to make a stem.

Always take the greatest care when using carmine powder. It stains easily and the slightest draught will blow it around. Always wear an overall, and only use the powder for very special work. Never use sugar paste for carmine-powdered roses, as it is not suitable for holding a stem. For the basket-of-roses cakes (see page 62) it is not necessary to put a wire stem on the roses.

A wheelbarrow (made from pastillage) filled with roses modelled from almond paste.

A cake decorated with poinsettia made from coloured almond paste or sugar paste.

Making holly from almond paste.

Poinsettia

These flowers are very spectacular and make especially good decorations for Christmas cakes. Use red-coloured almond paste or red sugar paste. Cut a pattern in paper, copied from a real flower or picture. Roll out the paste thinly and place the pattern on the paste. Cut out with a sharp knife. Model with the fingers using a little cornflour. Press petals together. Make an arrangement with the flowers on the cake top.

Daffodil

Use almond paste or modelling fondant, coloured yellow. Roll out thinly with a rolling pin, using cornflour on the board. With a natural flower, or a good picture as a guide, cut a strip suitable for the width of a daffodil trumpet. Mould this around the fingers, and work in the join until it disappears. For each flower, cut six petal shapes with a knife. Shape and press thinly at the edges. Arrange in position on waxed paper, using folded tissue paper to lift the petals slightly to form a natural shape. Moisten the base of the trumpet and set it in position. Prop with tissue paper until firm.

Holly

Colour a little almond paste red and roll into tiny berries the size of a lentil. Colour the remainder of the paste green, but do not attempt to make the almond paste dark green like real holly. Roll out the green almond paste very thinly on a board lightly dredged with cornflour, and cut into strips $\frac{1}{4}$ inch ($\frac{1}{2}$ cm.) wide. Cut off the end of the strip like ribbon cut on the cross. Continue cutting diagonally down the strip, producing several diamond shapes.

Put the first finger of the right hand on top of one of the diamond shapes, and with a skewer, push in the point on one side of the diamond. Push in also above and below the point. Repeat on the other side. Repeat pushing on the first side if necessary. Mark the centre with a knife to represent the vein of the leaf. A No. 1 or 2 icing tube may also be used as a cutter to produce the shape of the holly leaf instead of the pushing method.

When the leaves and berries are dry, store them in an airtight tin. At Christmas time arrange them on a chocolate yule log or a cake, with a few almond paste stems. A tiny dab of water from an artist's paint brush can be used to moisten the leaves and berries to fix them in position. Ivy leaves and mistletoe can be made in the same way, using the natural coloured almond paste for berries.

Fruits *Illustrated on page 31*

Almond paste fruits can be used either as a decoration on a cake, as sweetmeats, or for serving as petits fours after a meal. As a decoration on a cake, they should be much smaller than for petits fours or sweets. Small pieces of left-over almond paste can be modelled into different fruits for cake decoration and kept in an airtight container to prevent them from becoming hard.

Apples Use natural-coloured, bought or home-made almond paste. After washing the hands – almond paste easily picks up any dust and becomes soiled – roll a small ball of almond paste. Make a slight indentation in the top and base. Using some red food colouring diluted with water, and an artist's fine paint brush, colour the almond paste apple realistically on one side, blending the colour to a paler shade. Similarly, paint the other side green, blending the red and green slightly, rubbing in the colours until they merge gently. Using scissors, cut a clove in two, and place one piece in the apple to represent the stem, and the other as the calyx.

Pears Make these similarly to apples. Begin with a suitably sized ball, about $\frac{3}{4}$ inch ($1\frac{1}{2}$ cm.) across, bringing up one side to a pear shape by working it round in the fingers. Use the same method of colouring as for apples.

Bananas Use a long, square, ridged shape; paint with food colouring in yellow and green with touches of brown.

Oranges and lemons Form a good shape first, and then mark the outside with a pin head or roll on a grater to form the texture of the surface peel. Colour orange and yellow.

Strawberries After shaping and colouring, roll in granulated sugar to give the seed effect. A green hull can be made from almond paste.

Peaches Shape and colour, and mark a line on one side with a knife.

Place the finished fruits in small paper cases in an attractive box. If liked, add a few leaves modelled in green almond paste, and use the fruits to decorate a cake – see the picture on page 31.

Model of a windmill covered with almond paste. The sails are made from royal icing piped on to wire.

Vegetables
Cauliflowers, cabbages, carrots, turnips – each one can be copied and makes a novel decoration.

Houses
Make a small oblong of almond paste $1\frac{1}{4}$ inches (3 cm.) long by $\frac{3}{4}$ inch ($1\frac{1}{2}$ cm.) wide. Build up to a pointed ridge. Colour some almond paste green or red and roll out an oblong to cover the ridge. Represent tiles by marking lines with a knife. Fix the roof to the house with jam. Pipe tiny doors and windows. With experience, even quite elaborate buildings can be modelled.

Birds' nests
Shape a small piece of almond paste into a ball, hollowing out the centre and pressing into the shape of a bird's nest. Colour

An almond paste model of a house.

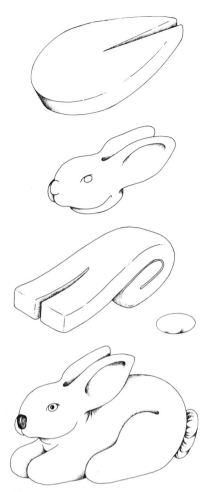

Making a model of a rabbit from almond paste.

some royal icing straw colour or brown, and with a No. 1 tube, pipe strands of icing over the nest and around the edges. Make several tiny almond paste eggs, colour some blue, and make some spotted, and place them in the nest. Model a bird – chicken, robin, thrush etc. – or buy a yellow cotton wool chick.

These nests are most generally used to decorate a Simnel cake, but for an even more unusual effect, make some small round cakes in bun tins, and place one of these nests on each cake. This makes a different and very popular Easter novelty.

Animals *Illustrated on page 26*

For these, the almond paste must be just the right consistency, neither too dry, nor too soft. If it is dry, add a little glucose or glycerine; if soft, add a little icing sugar.

To make a rabbit, form the almond paste into a roll about a finger's thickness. Cut off a piece and form into an oval for the head. Shape into a cone with a point at one end, and cut down the point with scissors to make the rabbit's ears.

Bend under one end of the almond paste roll and curve round to form the body and back legs. With scissors, cut the other end of the roll to form two front legs. Complete the shaping with fingers and thumb, and fix the head in position with a little egg white. When set firm, make two dots of white royal icing for the eyes, and centre each dot with a tiny blob of chocolate icing.

Pigs, mice, chickens and birds can be made in the same way. They are all especially popular at children's parties. Colour the animals using an artist's fine brush and food colouring.

From these basic instructions, almost any idea can be achieved for Christmas, birthday or any special occasions.

A Christmas cake covered with royal icing. The candle and holly are made from almond paste.

Candles

For the candle to lie flat on the cake roll out the coloured almond paste and cut to the size required with a knife. The top of the candle should be cut slightly on the slope to look more natural. Pipe some royal icing at the top to represent wax and pipe in the wick. A little icing dripping down one side gives a realistic effect. Colour the royal icing using a fine brush, with food colouring to match the candle. For the candle to stand up on the cake make a roll of almond paste cut to the required length and reinforce it with a piece of rustless wire. The piece of paste may also be made with a half round effect.

Royal icing

Royal icing is the special occasion icing. It is hard setting, and is always used for wedding cakes and some birthday cakes. It is the best kind of icing for piping designs and sugar flowers.

Always take special care and a little extra time when making royal icing so that a perfect dazzling whiteness is produced.

Equipment for royal icing

It is most essential to ensure that all the utensils used – bowls, measures, spoons, spatulas, etc., are clean and free from grease. When making royal icing for the first time, choose, if possible, a new white earthenware or porcelain bowl, about 10 inches (26 cm.) across the top, with a good glaze. This basin should be used for icing only, kept perfectly clean, and stored in a bag when not in use. Never use a cracked or crazed bowl, or one which has been used for creaming butter and sugar or steaming puddings, or the icing will discolour.

To be sure that the bowl used is absolutely clean, rub it well with salt, place all the utensils inside, and fill with boiling water to sterilise it. Leave to stand for a few minutes, and then rinse well. Allow to dry and cool with the bowl turned upside down. Even drying the bowl with a tea towel can spoil the icing, as a thread from the cloth may be inadvertently left behind and block the icing tube, so that the icing breaks when piping fine lines. This is annoying and causes bad workmanship when piping.

If it is intended to do a lot of cake decoration, a good quality turntable will be very useful and worth buying, but for home use, two inverted soup plates on top of each other can be used. To make an amateur turntable, use a round metal or tin tray about 12 inches (30 cm.) across, and two pieces of hard wood – two circular wooden teapot stands would be suitable. Make an identical circular groove in both stands and place several ball-bearings in one of them. Place the two stands together with the ballbearings held in position between the grooves. Fasten the stands with a suitable screw, having made a slightly larger hole in the upper stand to enable it to rotate freely. A washer should be placed under the screw head before assembling. Finally, drill four holes in the tray and screw it upside down on to the upper teapot stand. Any handyman should be able to do this.

Care of sugar

Icing sugar should be bought in sealed packages and stored in a dry place, not in a kitchen cupboard where there may be steam. Lumpy sugar is unsatisfactory, as sifting and rolling to remove lumps may make the sugar greasy or soiled and discolour the icing, preventing that perfect whiteness so essential on a good cake. A packet of lumpy icing sugar can always be used up for making glacé icing for a sponge or sandwich cake, but not for royal icing.

Immediately after using the icing sugar, close up the packet and store it in a dry place. The manufacturers go to much trouble preparing, packing and sealing icing sugar – the user should take a similar amount of care. One speck of dust in the sugar can ruin the beautiful whiteness of a wedding cake and take away the 'untouched by hand look' that home-made cakes and sweets should have to raise them above the level of manufactured goods.

To mix royal icing

Having carefully prepared the bowl and utensils, put the egg white into the bowl first. Instead of pure egg white, it is possible to use a reconstituted substitute (Hyfoama, Icine, Merriwhite etc.) or even gelatine soaked and dissolved in water. Using a substitute solves the problem of surplus egg yolks. Gradually add the icing sugar straight from the freshly opened packet, without sifting.

It is not possible to give the correct weight of sugar to each egg, as some eggs are naturally much larger than others, some people are much more clever than others at extracting all the white from an egg, and some icing jobs need stiffer icing, and therefore more sugar than others. However, generally it may help to know that:

1 egg white will take 4–8 oz. (100–225 g.) icing sugar

or 1 teaspoon powdered substitute to 4 tablespoons cold water will take about 1 lb. (450 g.) sugar

or $\frac{1}{4}$ oz. (10 g.) gelatine to 4 tablespoons water will take about 1 lb. (450 g.) sugar

If a little yolk should get into the white when breaking an egg, it should never be used for making royal icing. It can be used for cake making, or for family use, but another egg white must be used for the icing.

Stir or beat the egg white and icing sugar thoroughly with a flat wooden spatula, using a vigorous stirring movement rather than actually beating. Add the sugar and beat well until the mixture is like thick, unwhipped cream. At this stage it should pour heavily from the spoon or spatula. Continue stirring vigorously until the icing is stiff enough and will stand in a peak. It may be necessary to add a little more sugar, but the more it is beaten, the stiffer the icing should become. If too much sugar is added and not enough beating done, the icing will be short, hard to pipe, and hard on the cake to cut and eat.

It is not considered possible to over-beat royal icing by hand – the accepted time is usually about 20 minutes. It is possible to take a rest halfway through, and then to resume beating, but in the meantime, the icing should be covered with a damp cloth, wrung out in clean, cold water.

If an electric mixer is used, it should be run on a slow speed for about 4 minutes only, or until the icing becomes the required

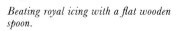

Beating royal icing with a flat wooden spoon.

stiffness. When making icing in a machine, take care to see that it is not over-beaten. This causes pockets of air, and produces fluffy icing which, if used for coating the top of a cake, will form a rough, bubbly surface instead of a smooth one, and will cause piping to break frequently because of the air in the sugar. Avoid using an egg whisk for the same reasons. To even up the texture of icing made on a mixer, spend a few seconds re-beating the icing with a wooden spoon.

If an egg substitute is used in the machine, put 1 teaspoon, or the required amount of powder into the 1 lb. (450 g.) of dry icing sugar, and stir together before adding to the water already in the mixer. Again, the bowl of the machine must be sterilised before making royal icing, as it will undoubtedly have been used for making cakes and creaming fat. Although a porcelain or similar bowl is better than a metal one, the metal beater for the machine will have to be used, so make sure to scald it with boiling water before use.

For best results, separate fresh eggs the night before making the icing, and allow the whites to stand at room temperature, covered with a damp cloth.

As with everything else, perfect royal icing takes a lot of practice and a lot of patience, but the final effect is always worth the time taken. Stiff icing is suitable for stars and scroll work, a slightly softer icing for lines and writing. For covering a surface, use a softer icing still. If the icing is too stiff for surface work, thin it by adding a little more egg white – or water if a substitute albumen is used – and re-beating. If it is too soft, continue beating, and only add a little more sugar if absolutely necessary.

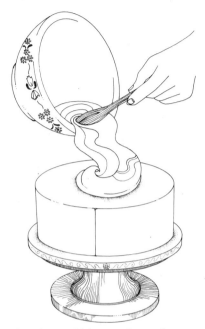

Spooning royal icing over the top of a fruit cake covered with almond paste.

To obtain a flat surface

A good, smooth, flat surface is very necessary for a cake with piping. When the almond paste on the cake has had two or three days to dry, put the cake – which should be on a silver board 2 inches (5 cm.) larger than the diameter of the cake – on a turn-table, or two inverted soup plates so that the cake can be easily turned round. Re-beat the royal icing to the correct coating consistency, and test by lifting the icing on a flat wooden spoon or spatula: it should pull up in a point on the spoon, but the point should easily fall over.

For a 7-inch (18-cm.) cake, place about a breakfastcupful of the royal icing in the centre of the cake and, with a palette knife, spread it evenly over the surface. Allow the icing to come over the sides and down to the base of the cake, using a backwards and forwards movement. Wipe the knife free from icing, and then hold it at the back of the cake, with the blade across the cake tilted at an angle of 45°, the point reaching slightly beyond the centre. Place the left hand also at the back of the cake holding the cake board, and begin turning slowly, moving the blade

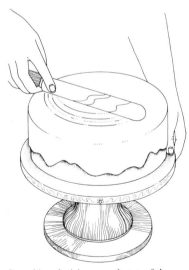

Smoothing the icing over the top of the cake with a palette knife using a back-wards and forwards movement. Allow the icing to cover the sides and down to the base of the cake.

46

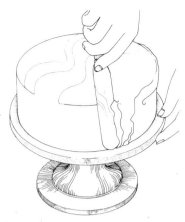

Smoothing the icing on the sides of the cake with a palette knife.

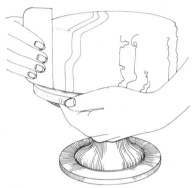

Taking a scraper around the sides of the cake to give a perfect finish.

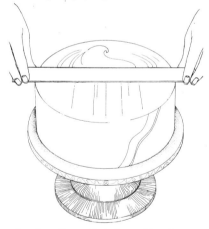

An alternative method of smoothing the icing on the surface of the cake using a steel ruler.

round with the right hand, and the board with the left, so that the icing is gradually smoothed over the surface and both hands eventually meet at the front of the cake, thus completing a circle. When the entire surface is smooth, quickly lift the knife. This leaves a take-off mark which is always present when learning to coat the surface of a cake. With experience, less take-off mark will be noticeable.

When the top surface is completed, place a plastic scraper or palette knife against the side of the cake. Again, starting at the back, with both hands together, turn the cake by its base with the left hand, smoothing the icing with the scraper in the right hand, making as little take-off mark as possible. If necessary, take the scraper around the sides of the cake several times but keep it at right angles to the silver board, and resting on it, so that the cake sides are perfectly upright. Replace any smoothed off icing in the bowl.

An alternative method of smoothing the surface is to take the knife or a smooth steel or plastic ruler across the top of the cake.

Whichever method is used, remove any surplus icing from the edge of the cake.

Allow the icing to dry for two or three days in a warm place, and then with fine sandpaper, rub down the take-off mark on the icing, and any other roughness on the surface. Holes which may appear can be filled with a little of the royal icing, and sand-papered smooth when dry – with more experience, this should not be necessary.

The first coat of royal icing should always be very thin as it is really only a key between the almond paste and the next coat of royal icing. Give the cake a second coat of icing in the same way as the first. Leave it in a warm place for two or three days to become quite dry, and, if necessary, use the sandpaper again to improve the surface. On special cakes, a third, or perhaps even a fourth coat of royal icing is usually necessary. Each coat gives a smoother, finer finish, but each must also be very thin, or the icing will be hard. All four coats together should not be more than $\frac{1}{8}$ inch ($\frac{1}{4}$ cm.) in thickness.

A good surface has beauty in itself, and does not require elaborate decoration. In fact, it is often the plainer designs that look the best, if they are neatly and well carried out. The icing should be quite firm and dry before any decorating is done, because if a mistake should occur, the fresh icing can be far more easily removed from a dry surface than a soft one. If possible, allow the surface to dry for about a week in a warm room, before piping the decoration. When dry, wrap the cake in foil until ready for decorating. When decorated, a box is necessary as foil would spoil the fine work. Store in a dry place as any dampness will spoil icing.

To make a softer royal icing, add 1 teaspoon glycerine to each

Removing any slight imperfections from the dry icing by rubbing the surface with fine sandpaper.

1 lb. (450 g.) icing sugar – this method, however, should never be used for exhibition or examination work, and is not advisable for wedding cakes, especially if pillars have to stand on the top surface to hold further tiers of cakes. If hard royal icing is placed in a room with a kettle of boiling water for a short while, the steam will make cutting easier, but even so, a good, suitable knife is necessary to cut it successfully.

It is always best to cut right across the centre of a royal-iced cake, and then cut 1-inch (2½-cm.) wide strips. Lay the strips on a board and cut into fingers. Never attempt to cut wedge pieces, as the fine point in the centre of the cake will always crumble and fall away.

To add colour to royal icing
Royal icing will take colour well for piping or for surfacing, although it is not advisable to use sandpaper on a coloured surface, as the sugar always remains in fine grains, and sand-papering divides the grains, showing the white sugar. It is possible, of course, to sandpaper the first coat of coloured icing, and then to top with a fresh un-sandpapered surface.

Coloured piping designs look attractive on white, but very strong colours should be used only with great care – particularly red, which is inclined to run, especially if there is any dampness in the atmosphere.

But for the uninitiated, white icing is always the safest way to success. To make sure of producing a really good white, laundry blue (or a drop of blue food colouring) is often added to white icing. Scrape only a small quantity from the block of laundry blue, and dissolve it in ½ teaspoon cold water. When the icing is mixed, beat in the blue liquid. It may be necessary to stiffen the icing again afterwards. Be careful not to add too much blue, as it can sometimes be difficult to regain a good white; however if this does happen, keep the cake for a long time, and the icing should eventually fade to a good white again. Badly made royal icing can become yellow through under-beating, or through lack of care of utensils. As previously stressed, any grease in the icing will spoil its texture and make it run and lose its shape. More sugar is added, and a bad icing becomes worse. Not only these faults, but drying too near heat and a foggy atmosphere can also cause white icing to turn yellowish.

Laundry blue should never be added to coloured icing.

To make a snow scene Christmas cake
Make a firm cake, preferably a fruit one, with a flat top – cut to make a good surface if the cake has risen slightly in baking. Cover carefully with almond paste, and place on a thick silver board, 2 inches (5 cm.) larger than the diameter of the cake. Allow to dry for a day or two, and then make a stiff royal icing. 8 oz. (225 g.)

A snow scene cake in royal icing.

icing sugar will cover an 8-inch (20-cm.) cake. Use more icing sugar if using gelatine icing. If liked, the top and the sides of the cake may be flat iced first and allowed to dry.

Spoon all the icing on to the cake and coat the top and sides, if liked. With a dry knife, pull up the icing roughly all over to form points, and perhaps smooth one side to set flat for writing greetings, or painting in a scene.

To decorate, make a model of Santa Claus or a reindeer and if liked, sprigs of holly and mistletoe. A collar (see page 145) may be put on the cake and a red ribbon tied around the sides. The edge of the cake board should either be cleaned with a damp cloth to remove any icing which may have fallen on to it – this must be done at once, before the icing sets hard – or spread with a thin layer of icing and roughed up.

Decoration with a serrated scraper *Illustrated on page 91*
Apart from the snow method, a quick and attractive surface can also be obtained by using a serrated scraper. Coat with a thin layer of royal icing as evenly as possible over the almond paste, and allow to set in a dry place for two or three days. Coat again with well beaten icing, stiff enough to stand up in points, as for the snow scene. Using the serrated scraper, mark round the top and sides in rings or patterns. The board may be decorated too.

Fan-like patterns can be made by using the scraper with a semi-circular movement, or cobweb designs by moving it convexly –

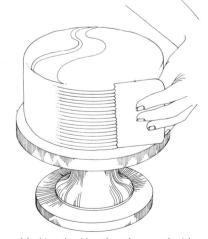

Marking the sides of a cake covered with royal icing with a serrated scraper.

A wedding buffet. The royal iced cake is decorated with a simple design using an eight-point star template as a guide.

A good surface in royal icing simply decorated with shells and piped flowers. Cut a template to make the loops around the sides even.

Another simple, but effective, design for a wedding cake decorated with roses made from sugar paste or pastillage.

variations grow as experience is gained. Any take-off mark can be hidden with a decorative spray of flowers or holly.

Leave the cake to dry, and decorate the top and bottom edges with piped stars, or lace pieces.

To practise royal icing

To reach the perfection seen on professionally iced cakes is one of the most difficult jobs in cake decoration. Practice is so important that it is a good plan to make a cake model to work on. Find a suitable tin with a flat lid, about 7 inches (18 cm.) in diameter. Place the tin on a thick silver cake board or cake drum, place a small block of wood inside, and insert a screw up from under the silver board, through the tin, and into the wood. Put the lid on the tin, and practise icing it, just like a cake. As well as practising icing flat surfaces, try out designs with the serrated scraper in this way, too. The icing can be scraped off the tin when the practice is over, and kept covered with a damp cloth, in a screw-top jar or in an airtight polythene container, until there is time to practise again; the icing will, of course, have to be re-beaten before use.

This is the only way to become proficient. There are never enough real cakes to accommodate all the practice that every amateur cake decorator needs.

When royal icing is not in use, it should be covered with a damp cloth and kept damp all the time, to prevent the icing from drying. If it is to be kept for day-to-day practice, the cloth must be washed out daily and dried in the open air, a second cloth being used in the meantime.

The art of royal icing needs constant practice, perfect cleanliness, and a lot of attention and patience. It is the really professional icing, and there is no easy short cut to success.

The bowl containing royal icing must always be kept covered with a damp tea towel to prevent the icing from drying out.

To pipe designs

Piping is a fascinating art. The simplest designs can be easily executed, and the most intricate designs can be carried out from the instructions given. But to achieve any worthwhile result, as with all else in the art of cake decorating, there is only one road to success: to practise.

Because practice is so all-important, it is best to provide ample facilities for practising before attempting to begin to learn piping. As a model cake surface helped in practising to ice a smooth surface, so a practice board will help towards practising piped designs.

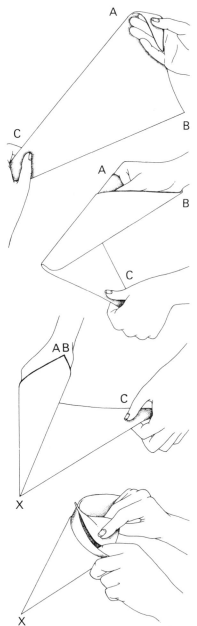

Making an icing bag from greaseproof paper.

To make a practice board

Cover a thick silver cake board with one of the many kinds of self-adhesive plastic coverings used for lining shelves. If the bottom of the board is covered with the plastic covering – plain colours, yellow, brown or blue, are best – the silver side can still be used as a cake board. Patterned surfaces are difficult to pipe on to without straining the eyes. If old boards do become untidy, the silver paper for re-covering them is available.

Once the practice board is made, keep it for trying out designs before working on the actual cake, for practising the balance of a proposed design, and the arrangement of lettering and sugar flower sprays.

To make a piping bag

Paper bags made with greaseproof paper are usually far the best for royal icing. Metal icing sets or pumps are available, but are difficult to control. Icing bags made of calico are apt to make the hands sticky, and plastic or nylon bags require careful washing. On the whole, paper icing bags are less wasteful and far less trouble.

Using the best quality greaseproof paper – sheets usually measure about 30 inches (78 cm.) by 20 inches (52 cm.) – fold one sheet in half, then in half again and again. Open out. The sheet is now divided into eight oblongs, all 10 inches (26 cm.) by $7\frac{1}{2}$ inches (19 cm.). Cut out these oblongs and cut each one across diagonally, from corner to corner, making sixteen triangles of paper, sufficient for sixteen icing bags, with no wastage of greaseproof paper.

To make the icing bags, hold one of the paper triangles with the longest side on the left, and the shortest side at the top. With the right hand, in the paper, take hold of point A. Bring point A to point B and take point C forward and then round the back to meet A and B, forming a cone with the point at X. There should be no hole at the point X, and X should be a sharp point. If there is any hole at X, adjust carefully, pulling the long point of paper.

An attractive design for a wedding cake, using an eight-point star template with slightly rounded hollows as a guide. Braiding helps to make the design stand out; the roses are modelled from pastillage.

A Christmas cake. The scene is painted on the flat surface with food colouring and an artist's fine brush. The standing Christmas trees around the top edge are run-out and piped on to pieces of waxed paper.

Make the bag secure by folding in the long point.

Only make enough bags for immediate use, as storing can flatten and crease the points.

To fill a bag with icing

For practice work, about half an egg white can be kept aside from the general daily cookery, and stored in a screw-top jar or covered with a damp cloth. To the egg white add enough icing sugar to make a stiff icing when well beaten – stiff enough to pull up into peaks.

Hold the bag in the left hand with the thumb on the outside. Take up some of the royal icing on a thin kitchen knife, not a wide palette knife, draw the icing in a long point, and place the point of icing down into the bag. Bring the knife against the left thumb, pressing the icing off the knife. Do not press the bag together, as a second amount of icing may have to be put into the bag, and even a third if necessary. Take care not to over-fill the bag, as this can cause the icing to come out at the top, or the bag to burst. Fold over the bag carefully at the top and press the icing down towards the point. Then fold the sides down on the top to give a flat, cushion-like rest for the thumb.

Before beginning to pipe, it will be necessary to cut the point off the bag to make a small hole – only use metal nozzles after some practice with the paper icing bag alone. For fine line work, cut about $\frac{1}{16}$ inch ($\frac{1}{8}$ cm.) from the bag. It is important to make this cut at right angles to the bag, and not on the slant. This cut should give a hole equal to the No. 1 writing tube.

From now on, the basin of icing must be kept covered with a wet cloth. If the paper cone is carefully unfolded, any icing from a finished bag can be scraped back into the bowl. Re-beat before filling each bag. Avoid the temptation to eat the icing. Special care must be paid to hygiene, and finger-licking must not be allowed. Keep a damp sponge ready for wiping the hands.

Filling an icing bag with royal icing.

To begin piping

A beginner should start by practising straight lines on to the practice board or the back of a plate. Hold the paper icing bag with the fingers at the side, and press with the thumb only on the flat, folded paper cushion at the top. Practise for some time before attempting to work on a cake. In fact, however proficient, it is always a good idea to try out the size of the hole cut in the piping bag before beginning to work on a cake.

With the point of the bag just touching the plate or practice board, press gently with the thumb. Watch the work carefully all the time. Move on as soon as the icing starts to come from the bag, making a smooth line. If a knob occurs, it is either because the icing is being pressed from the bag before it is in contact with the practice board, or else the movement is not quick enough.

56

The beginner will soon learn to regulate the pressure on the icing bag and to balance the rate of movement, so that just enough icing is pressed out to make the line even.

It is also important to finish without a knob. When the end of the line of icing is nearly reached, release the thumb pressure and lay down the icing, touching the board to break it off.

If the finished line is wavy, the pressure has been too great. If the line breaks, the pressure has been too little. To become expert, continue making lines until perfect. If the line twists, raise the icing bag more. The line of piping coming from the bag should always be about $\frac{1}{2}$–1 inch (1–2$\frac{1}{2}$ cm.) above the practice board. Do not be afraid to lift the work – a straighter line will be obtained this way, and any twists in the icing line will have time to straighten out before it is laid down on the design. It is not lifting that breaks a line, but insufficient pressure. Always pipe towards oneself whenever possible, never backwards.

As a change from making straight lines, try writing, and making a row of dots. This is good practice for starting and stopping. To make dots, touch the board and raise quickly, using hardly any pressure. When writing, touch, then lift the line of piping and allow the icing to run from the bag. Do not try to keep the bag on the board all the time. Touch again to break off.

To use icing tubes or nozzles

After really thorough practice with the paper bag only, try using an icing tube. A No. 1 plain tube is suitable for lines and gives a continual, even line, whereas the bag eventually wears out at the point, and cannot make an even thickness of line for any length of time.

Cut off about $\frac{1}{2}$ inch (1 cm.) of paper from the end of the bag, and insert the tube. Make sure it comes through the hole sufficiently as the end of the paper bag can interfere with the shape of the icing, particularly when using a star tube. To fill the bag, hold it in the left hand, as before, but take extra care not to allow the icing to escape between the tube and the bag by disturbing the close fit of the tube.

Never press on to the practice board so hard that the tube is pushed back into the bag. This would allow the icing to seep down between the bag and the tube, and present enormous difficulties. Apart from this hazard, piping lines with a metal tube is much the same as piping with the bag alone.

For more practice, try making dots with the writing tube – by pushing out more icing, a bigger dot is formed. Make graduated dots, remembering all the time to hold the bag at right angles above the board. Press gently, giving only one squeeze. Stop pressing and raise the bag quickly. Gradually increase the size of the dot by exerting greater pressure on the bag and raising it quickly.

Making a series of dots with an icing bag and a No. 1 tube. Thorough practice is essential to obtain a good standard in piping designs.

A triangular cake, to represent a Christmas tree, decorated with a trellis pattern in royal icing. The base is covered with sugar paste.

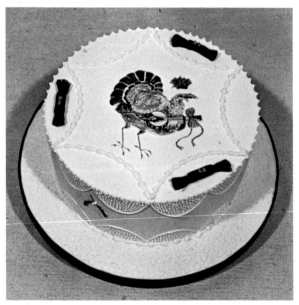

A Christmas cake decorated with a six-point star pattern and a traditional turkey painted on the cake surface with food colouring.

A Christmas cake decorated with a figure of Santa Claus painted on a pastillage plaque. Curtain work surrounds the plaque; the curtain work is repeated on the board.

A cake decorated with a Christmas design of a painted figure, old English lettering and trellis bells.

A neat design worked on a round cake, with braiding on the board.

An attractive edging for a Christmas cake. The rings are piped on to waxed paper and, when set, fixed on to the cake, then the continuous lines are piped on.

A sugar basket worked in royal icing to hold sweets, or fresh strawberries for à dessert (see page 121). A corner of freehand piped Wedgwood work is also shown.

A cake piped with lines and stars. A No. 1 tube is used for the lines and a No. 5 tube for the stars.

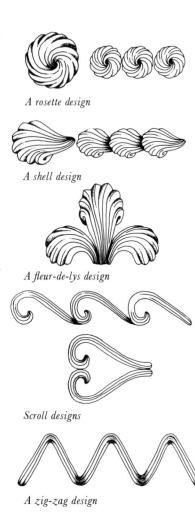

A rosette design

A shell design

A fleur-de-lys design

Scroll designs

A zig-zag design

To use a star tube

A No. 5 star tube is useful to have, although larger star tubes with the same number or more points are needed for more advanced work. A No. 5 tube has eight points and makes a neat star. Star tubes vary from a No. 5 to a No. 15. A larger star of icing can be made with a small star tube by pressing more icing from the bag, but a smaller star cannot be made with a larger tube. Bear this in mind and buy the smaller star tube to begin with.

Making stars is almost the same as making dots. Insert the tube into the bag. Use very stiff icing to avoid a point – a good star should be made without a point. Hold the tube at right angles to the cake or board, almost touching it, and press out some icing. Raise the tube quickly. Practise making large or small stars, all with the same tube, by pressing out more or less icing.

Vary the practice by buying small 2p-sized biscuits, or making them using a cocktail cutter, and icing each one with a star. This makes a good practice exercise and is interesting as well – especially if the icing is coloured with a few drops of food colouring. These small star biscuits are perfect for a children's party. If the icing stars are made on waxed paper they can be served as children's sweets. Alternatively, for a cocktail party, beat some soft cream cheese and pipe stars on to savoury biscuits. Sprinkle with chopped parsley.

Designs using a star tube

To make a rosette Press out the icing and move around in a circle towards the centre, completely enclosing the middle; pull off quickly to avoid leaving a point.

To make a shell Hold a star tube on its side, press lightly and move slightly back, then forward; pressing, pull off quickly.

To make a fleur-de-lys Make a centre shell with a slightly longer end to finish. Pipe out another shell a little to the left moving in a circle and down and in towards the centre shell. Pull off quickly. Add another shell on the right of the centre shell. This time circle more towards the centre and down. Pull off quickly to match the other side.

To make a scroll Work a question mark shape with a thin long tail ending in a point to break off. To form a border work the second scroll on to the tail of the first and continue for the length required. Also make left- and right-hand scrolls and fit them together.

To make a zig-zag border For this border, work a zig-zag line, bringing the line forward and up pressing evenly.

To use a fine writing tube

Touch the practice board, press out the icing and immediately it touches the board lift the tube, at the same time pressing so

Writing with a No. 1 tube. Begin and end neatly without a knob.

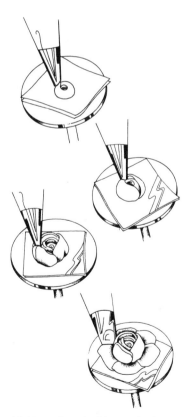

Making a flower, with a petal tube, on an icing nail. The flower is worked on a small square of waxed paper secured to the nail with a dot of icing.

that the icing will flow out in a thin line. Move the hand along and make a straight line of icing. Too much pressure will cause the icing to wobble and if too little is exerted the icing line will break. With practice the lines will be quite straight and even. Touch the board or cake again to break off without a knob.

To make dots Work as described on page 57; touch the surface, holding the tube in the bag perpendicular to the board and lift off quickly. For a larger dot press out more icing. There should be no point on the dot and unless making graduated dots, they should be even in size in the one row.

To write Work as for lines, printing the letters first. Begin neatly (without a knob), touch the surface, lift off and finish well. After practice, handwriting can be tried; there is no end to the fancy lettering which can be used as decoration on a cake. Study the inscriptions on some of the pictures in this book.

To use a ribbon tube

Start as for making a line by just touching the board and press out the icing. Lift and move along, touch to break off. Loops, bows and zig-zag borders can be made with this tube.

To use a petal tube

This tube is primarily used for making flowers, but it may also be used for border work and frilling.

Begin by touching the board, having the hollow of the tube uppermost and work in a fan movement and pull off quickly for each petal; use the tube level with the board when making petals. Practise making single petals and then scrape the icing back into the bowl; beat well and keep covered with a damp cloth for use again. Now try making six petals in a circle to form a flower, then make dots in another colour in the centre for the stamens. Alternatively, work on a flower nail with a small square of waxed paper on top. Secure the waxed paper square to the nail with a dot of icing. When proficient at making flowers, pipe out a number and store them carefully in a box for future use. See pages 77–80 for further instructions on making flowers.

To build up a design

Using a No. 1 icing tube, or a bag cut to the same size, pipe out the following design for a round cake. Make two tiny dots of icing opposite each other at the highest and lowest points on the edge of a round practice board. Turn the board a quarter-circle, and make a third and fourth dot at the points now highest and lowest on the circle. Make four more dots between those already made, marking eight equal spaces. Now make a second row of dots, 1 inch ($2\frac{1}{2}$ cm.) in from the edge of the board, and half-way between each of the previous dots. Make icing lines joining the dots, as in the drawing to form an eight-point star. Complete the

A basket cake with a handle containing almond paste roses. Royal icing is used for the basket work piping (see page 74).

A royal icing basket cake with almond paste roses (see page 74).

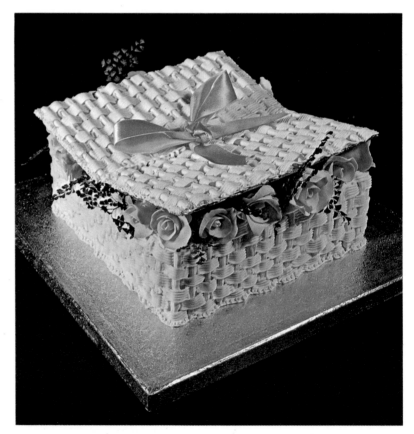

A square basket cake with a double lid piped in royal icing. The roses are made from almond paste (see page 39).

A fort cake, for a child's birthday, covered with sugar paste and decorated with royal icing. The cake mixture is baked in a square tin and cut to shape.

A crib scene covered with sugar paste. The figures are made from royal icing and sugar paste.

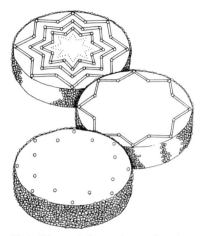

To build up a design on the top of a cake.

design with several more lines to form three eight-point stars inside each other and a row of dots as in the drawing.

To give the professional finish to this design, build it up by working a second line of piping on the middle star, and a second and third line of piping exactly on top of each other, on the outer star. Graduated dots give the finishing touch to the design.

In the drawings opposite, variations of the eight-point star pattern are shown. The marking dots are the same in each case, but the line work on each one gives a different design. These should all be practised as an exercise, and when perfected, can be piped in royal icing on to a sponge or sandwich cake with a flat top, previously iced with glacé icing and allowed to become quite set. Pale-coloured glacé icing with white royal piping, or white glacé icing and coloured piping look equally attractive. Left-over glacé icing can be used for piping by adding a small quantity of powdered albumen egg substitute. Beat the icing well to a suitable stiffness and texture for practice piping only. This type of cake, with this type of decoration, should be made and eaten the same day, as glacé icing softens the royal icing. Nevertheless, this is all good practice, and piping designs on to a cake often inspires far more interest than piping on to a practice board.

For further practice, try experimenting with more line designs – the wider the range of practice designs, the more interest will be held. With royal icing, make a straight line through the centre of the cake, from top to bottom. Turn the cake a quarter circle to the left, and make a second line from top to bottom, dividing the cake into quarters. Again turning the cake to the left, make a third line $\frac{1}{4}$ inch ($\frac{1}{2}$ cm.) to the right of the first line. Turn to the left again, and work a fourth line, on the right of the second line, and $\frac{1}{4}$ inch ($\frac{1}{2}$ cm.) from it. Continue making these lines $\frac{1}{4}$ inch ($\frac{1}{2}$ cm.) apart, always turning the cake to the left, and always piping the new line on the right of the existing lines, until the whole cake is covered.

If preferred, two colours can be used, in two tubes of the same thickness. Using pink, or blue, and white, keep the pink lines running next to each other, and the white lines running parallel to each other. Even three or four interlacing lines make a simple and attractive design on a glacé iced cake. It is not necessary to keep the lines central, and a small decoration, perhaps a glacé cherry, a nut, or some simple lettering, can fill the quarter space.

After some practice, a cake can be turned one-sixth, or one-eighth, and the lines crossed in the same way, producing a six- or eight-point star pattern of interlacing lines.

For variations, outline scrolls on a practice board with fine lines or dots, or over-pipe by building up lines on the scroll with a No. 1 tube. Improve on old ideas or search out new ones by looking at the pictures in this book, at the cakes in shop windows, and even by studying the scroll work on the ceilings in old houses.

To pipe decorations

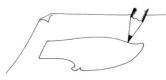

Drawing a pattern of the wing on greaseproof paper.

The pattern filled in with curved lines worked from A to B.

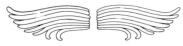

A completed pair of wings.

A completed tail.

The completed bird. The body is piped from an icing bag, cut to the size of a No. 4 tube, starting at the tail end and pulling off quickly to form the beak.

Some of the most fascinating cakes to ice, and also those which give the most pleasure, are cakes with individual or topical designs and scenes. With patience and practice it is possible to produce the most intricate and specific scenes – a game of tennis for a twenty-first birthday cake for a sport enthusiast; a garden, a sea gull scene or a Christmas scene for children.

Begin by learning to make birds for decoration. These are perhaps the simplest of all figures to make, and can be used on almost any type of cake, even an ornate wedding cake.

To pipe birds

Icing for piping birds should be slightly softer than for piping lines or stars, and a paper bag is preferable to an icing tube, as this gives a softer line. Make a neat, firm bag, fill with well beaten icing, and fold down tidily, as it is necessary to have full control.

In the beginning, as a rough guide, draw a pattern of the wings on greaseproof paper using a coin to make a good curve. Cover the greaseproof with thin waxed paper so that the pattern can still be seen clearly. Cut the paper icing bag to the size of a No. 1 tube and work curved lines on to the waxed paper, beginning at point A and working backwards and forwards between A and B without lifting the tube, until the entire wing span is filled. Each line must be shorter than the previous one, and all must be touching each other or the wing will break. The inner edge must be straight, to insert into the bird's body, and the icing should resemble feathers.

Make the wings in pairs, left and right, and to each pair of wings, make a tail, either straight or fan-tailed according to the species of bird.

Leave the wings and tails until quite dry, and then remove them very carefully from the waxed paper. Until they are needed, keep in a box lined with cotton wool.

To make a bird's body, use a well beaten, stiff icing, and cut off the end of the icing bag to the same size as a No. 4 plain tube. Touch the waxed paper and press out a bulb of icing, keeping the point of the bag in one place all the time. When the bulb is slightly more than a $\frac{1}{4}$ inch ($\frac{1}{2}$ cm.) long, raise the bag a little to form the neck, and press again to form the head. Pull off very quickly to make the beak.

When a good body has been made, insert one of the dry sugar tails in the correct position, and a left and right wing, taking care that the curve done first – A to B – is at the head of the bird, otherwise the wings will be flying one way, and the body another!

When each bird is made, use a tiny piece of crushed tissue paper to prop up the tail and wings, and when quite dry, paint the beak yellow or orange with food colouring, and add two dark dots for eyes, using an artist's very fine brush. Store, still on the waxed paper, in a box lined with cotton wool until required. When proficient the body can be piped straight on to the cake and the dry wings and tail inserted. The body only can be made in yellow icing to represent ducks.

To design a sea scene *Illustrated on page 19*

A Madeira, sponge or sandwich cake is the most suitable cake for this type of icing scene.

Make some glacé icing using about 1 oz. (25 g.) icing sugar for every 1 inch (2½ cm.) of the diameter of the cake. Spread the sides of the cake with a little glacé icing, roll in toasted almonds or coconut, and place the cake on a doily on a serving plate.

Colour the remaining icing pale blue, and coat the entire top of the cake, just to the edge. Leave to set. Using a bag only, or a No. 1 tube, pipe wavy lines of white royal icing across one-third of the cake, to represent the sea. Add a freehand lighthouse, clouds, flying birds and, if the cake surface is large enough, a yacht. This is essentially a quick cake, so only the outlines are necessary simply to convey the idea, rather than a full-scale intricate, artistic picture. When the rest of the scene is set, place the sugar birds already made in position on the waves. When making this scene for the first time, try it out on the practice board.

If necessary, the cake can be neatened around the top edge, by piping with the bag cut with a large hole as for the birds' bodies. Pipe round bulbs of white royal icing about the size of a pea, touching each other all around the edge of the cake. Allow to dry, and finally add a little powdered albumen substitute to the blue icing that is left; beat well and using a No. 1 tube join two of the bulbs by over-piping a letter 's' around every two bulbs of icing. This must be neatly done, and gives good practice in over-piping which is needed for more advanced work.

To pipe birds on to a cake surface

Sometimes flying birds have to be piped, side-view, on to the side of a cake, and it is impossible to make both wings and the tail on waxed paper first. In this case, pipe one wing on to the waxed paper and leave it to dry. Pipe the second wing straight on to the cake in the right position and, using another bag with a large hole, pipe the body and head of the bird as described previously, but sideways, bringing off the beak near the cake. Reverting to the finer bag, pipe in the tail and then insert the other wing, which should be quite dry. If the body icing is firm but not dry, the wing should stay well in position. Paint the beak and eye with food colouring.

With more experience it is possible to shade the birds, using dark and light greys to give reality to the gulls' wings.

These basic ideas can be used for making most other species. Colour the icing black to make blackbirds, blue for bluebirds, or brown for sparrows. To make a robin, pipe a little red icing on to

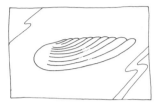

A wing piped on to waxed paper for a flying bird.

The body, wing and tail of a bird which would be piped straight on to the surface of a cake.

The wing, previously piped on to waxed paper, inserted in position.

A completed flying bird.

the breast of a brown bird. When the birds have been perfected, store them carefully in a dry, safe place for future use.

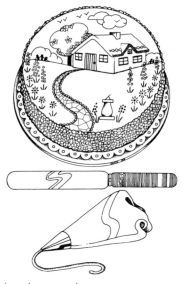

A garden scene cake.

To design a garden scene

This is an ideal design for a small tea party. It should be used on a sandwich, Madeira or genoese cake and eaten the same day it is made as these decorations will not keep well.

Make up some glacé icing (about 8 oz. (225 g.) for an 8-inch (20-cm.) cake). Spread a little icing around the sides of the cake, then coat the sides with toasted nuts or chocolate vermicelli. Place the cake on a serving plate with a doily. Colour half of the icing pale blue and half pale green. Ice to an indefinite line halfway across the top surface of the cake with the pale blue icing. Leave to set, then ice the remaining lower half of the cake with some of the pale green icing, spreading it to meet the pale blue icing. Cover the remaining green icing with a damp cloth.

When this surface is set, make brown icing by adding cocoa powder to the remaining green icing, and mix to the right consistency for piping by adding a little more water or cocoa powder. Pipe a line representing a road, running along the join of the green and blue icing. Add a second line on the green icing, to form a converging road. Pipe a house, freehand, and make any tree trunks, crazy paving, or fences, and perhaps a small sundial. Make clouds with white royal icing, and a few daisies in the green grass, using tiny lines for petals. Colour a little icing pink or yellow, and pipe more flowers into the garden, using tiny dots for delphiniums and hollyhocks, and adding roses around the house and a little green icing to complete the trees. The effect should be quite realistic. If necessary, copy a picture, including archways, gates, or even be more ambitious and outline the house first, and then fill in just to the piping line. The sundial and flowers can be made on waxed paper before placing in position, but most intricate work is better on a royal iced cake, and it will keep far longer. As a final touch, add some tiny brown birds.

To design a tennis cake

This is definitely a novelty cake, enormously popular at a tennis party tea, or as a birthday cake for a keen tennis player.

Bake a Madeira, light cherry, sultana or coconut cake in a loaf or roasting tin with sloping sides. Hollow out the centre of the mixture before baking to obtain a level surface. If the surface of the cake is not quite level when baked, trim the surface and turn the cake upside down. Coat the sides with pale green icing and dip in pale green coconut. Place ready for icing on a silver board or on a doily on a plate, and try to avoid moving the cake after it has been iced. Use pale green icing for the top surface.

Measure the sides of the cake, and draw this size on to a piece of paper. Mark out the lines of a tennis court, leaving about

A cake decorated in a tennis court design, with glacé icing.

1 inch (2½ cm.) each end, and ½ inch (1 cm.) spare on the sides of the paper. When the correct basic idea has been planned out and is well in mind, pipe the lines on to the cake in white royal icing. Dye a little strip of butter muslin with some of the green food colouring. Iron it out, cut to the correct size for a net, and attach each end to a cocktail stick with royal icing. Place this across the lines of the tennis court in the correct position. Pipe a line of white icing along the top of the net.

Small plastic dolls can be used for figures, or follow the instructions for making run-out figures (see page 141). If liked, pipe tennis rackets lying on the grass, and perhaps a few balls on the court, made with a large dot of soft royal icing.

A cake decorated with a quilting pattern in glacé icing.

To make a quilting pattern

Cover a cake with royal or glacé icing over almond paste, to make a good surface. If the top surface is covered with glacé icing, the sides should be coated with icing and chopped nuts first. Using a No. 1 tube and white royal icing, pipe a line across the centre of the cake. Continue piping lines parallel to this central line, and 1 inch (2½ cm.) apart. Now turn the cake through one-eighth of a circle to the left and again make a line through the centre, crossing the first line at an angle of about 45°. Make parallel lines, again 1 inch (2½ cm.) apart so that a diamond pattern is formed.

To complete the design, make small green leaves at each intersection, and add little pink rosebuds by working a tiny circle of pink royal icing between each leaf.

A music cake.

To design a music cake

Use an oblong or square Madeira or light fruit cake and cover with sugar paste. Pipe with royal icing, using the picture as a guide and mould any additional decorations from almond paste. Run-out figures may be placed on the sides.

Feather icing

This design always has a professional effect, but is actually very easy to carry out. A Victoria sandwich cake is the most suitable basis, and the work should be done quickly before the icing has time to set.

As always, complete the sides of the cake and place on a plate with a doily. Before beginning to ice, make sure that all the ingredients and utensils are ready to hand: icing sugar, cocoa powder or instant coffee, hot water, greaseproof paper, icing bag, palette knife and skewer. Ice the top of the cake with white glacé icing, just thick enough to flow easily without running down the sides of the cake. Quickly add a little cocoa powder or instant coffee to the remaining icing and, if necessary, a little warm water. Put this into the ready-made icing bag.

Cut off the point of the bag, and pipe straight lines ½ inch

Feather icing a sponge cake with glacé icing. Other patterns can be seen on page 97.

(1 cm.) apart, across the whole of the top of the cake, beginning in the middle so that it is easier to pipe the lines parallel. Immediately the lines are completed, draw a skewer or knife point across them at right angles, again beginning in the middle. These skewer lines should be $\frac{3}{4}$ inch (2 cm.) apart. Turn the cake round and draw the skewer across again in between the first lines.

Allow the icing to set, then neaten the top edge by piping butter cream through a star tube. The stars or scrolls should be close together and placed on the edge of the cake, using the tube at right angles to the edge. Press out the right size star, and break off sharply. A second row of stars around the base of a cake gives a neat finish, and allows the cake to sit nicely on the dish.

To pipe simple borders
These borders are most suitable for royal iced cakes.

To pipe a floral border Use a No. 1 tube and pipe a wavy line with pale green icing. Pipe curved branches from the line and on these arrange small closed circles in coloured icing as flowers. Graduate the circles in size and finish the border with leaves made with the end of the bag cut to an inverted V.

To pipe a fan border Pipe even-sized small arcs and decorate each one with tiny loops. Over-pipe the arcs to give height. Arrange a dry piped flower in each space, then pipe a dot with five lines radiating from it below each arc to make a fan shape.

To pipe a scroll and flower border Pipe blue scrolls at regular intervals and place a dry pink flower on the scroll with a green leaf on each side; pipe a line of dots each side with a dot in between to give a lacy edge. Finish the border with a loop.

To pipe a butterfly border Pipe an 'e' shape in two continuous lines with green icing. Make a wide V, continuous and even, in the centre in chocolate brown icing. Finish with a circle of yellow with a green dot each side. Add a brown dot over each 'e', then pipe a butterfly in yellow icing with brown dots.

To pipe a forget-me-not border Pipe a row of pale rose coloured loops, about $\frac{1}{2}$ inch (1 cm.) in length. Pipe a second row in a deeper colour to come with the points between the first as in the drawing. Pipe blue six-dot forget-me-nots with a yellow dot centre evenly along the border and add a green stem and two leaves to each flower.

To pipe a hanging rose border This makes an attractive border for the side of a cake where roses are used on the top surface in a spray or posy. This pattern can be traced on thick paper and cut out and used as a template or guide to make sure the loops are even on the side of the cake. Have the loops in pale blue icing, with pink roses and green leaves.

To pipe a scroll border Use a No. 2 tube for this scroll. Press heavily at the start of the scroll and reduce the pressure as the tube is moved along. Pull off quickly leaving a pointed end.

A floral border

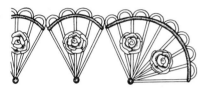

A fan border

A scroll and flower border

A butterfly border

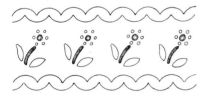

A forget-me-not border

A hanging rose border

A scroll border

To pipe designs on royal iced cakes

As experience is gained, more elaborate designs can be attempted, and these invariably need a certain amount of planning. All intricate piping patterns must first be worked out carefully before the design is carried out on the actual cake—for this purpose, it is useful to make several cardboard templates. This chapter deals with a few of the methods of producing a variety of accurate, complicated designs.

Before beginning to pipe a design, always make sure of a good surface by giving a cake two, three, or even more good coats of royal icing.

Never attempt to pipe any design on a royal iced cake until it is certain that the flat icing is completely dry.

To plan patterns for a round cake
It is possible to buy a set of marking rings or to make similar rings in cardboard, to help produce correct designs and evenly-spaced patterns. An equally good and sometimes simpler method is to cut a piece of greaseproof paper to the same size as the top of the cake using the cake tin as a guide. For patterns with eight points, fold this paper in half, in half again, and in half again, each time from the centre point. Keeping the paper folded, carefully fold once more, and with a soft pencil mark a straight line, as in the drawing from A to B. Cut through this line and open out. The paper should now be in the shape of an eight-point star. This provides a good basis for a variety of designs.

To design curved patterns
Again, cut the paper to the exact size of the cake top. Fold in the same way as described previously for an eight-point star, and mark with a pencil in a concave or a convex curve. Cut through the line to achieve the appropriate pattern.

For a six-point pattern, fold the paper in half, and then into three. Fold in half again to make sure that both sides of the curve will be even. The paper circle must be folded from the middle each time, and each fold must be perfectly straight and even.

To plan patterns for a square cake
Cut a piece of paper the same size as the top of the cake. Fold in half, in half again, and then diagonally to form a triangle. Each fold must come from the centre. Draw two pencil lines as in the drawing from A to B, and from B to C. Cut through the pencil line.

To vary these patterns, cut the paper in deeper or shallower curves, and use the basically round pattern on a square cake or vice versa. Try several patterns before deciding which one to use: make more folds, or alternate the point and the curve. Experiment by using one pattern inside another, perhaps placing the inner one off-centre.

Preparing the pattern for a round cake.

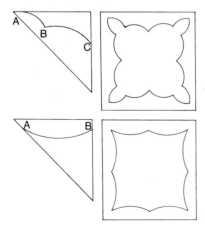

Preparing the pattern for a square cake.

A square cake decorated with a curved pattern. The pattern is first cut from greaseproof paper as described opposite.

To make a template

Once each paper pattern is completed, place it on a sheet of thin cardboard with no folds or creases in it, and outline carefully. Using sharp scissors, cut out the design in cardboard. Make a small V-shaped cut in the centre so that the template can easily be lifted from the cake later. Keep the templates to be used several times on different sized cakes.

How to use the template

This method is not practicable on soft icings such as butter cream or glacé icing, as the surface would immediately be spoiled. It is excellent for use on sugar paste or hard royal icing as a basic guide to complete accuracy.

When the icing is quite firm and dry, and the surface is as perfect as possible, place the template in position, folding up the V-shape ready for lifting. Pipe around the template, $\frac{1}{8}$ inch ($\frac{1}{4}$ cm.) from the edge of the cardboard, using a No. 1 or 2 icing tube. If the pattern is to be central, make sure that the points are all equidistant from the edge before beginning to pipe. Break the line of icing at each point in the design, and join again neatly. It is not wise to try to work round a point.

Take great care to make good curves – lift the icing to work round a curve, lowering the line of icing into position. Only practice will achieve this to perfection.

When the design is completed, carefully lift off the template, using the raised cut of cardboard in the centre as a handle. On a white surface always pipe the first lines in white. If a mistake occurs, white lines can easily be removed with a knife, and re-piped correctly. Coloured lines may leave a mark if they are removed. To complete the design, over-pipe in white or coloured icing.

Only the first line of piping around the template is needed before taking away the cardboard. Any further lines and decorations can be added freehand, parallel to the original design to give patterns inside one another. Emphasise the pattern by using tiny polka dots parallel to the first outline. Later, with more experience, pipe in lines of trellis, or groups of dots. But always, at first, practise the design on a practice board to achieve the correct balance and effect.

To make an eight-point star cake

The birthday cake in the picture opposite has the star pattern worked in white royal icing, with a second line of pale pink icing piped exactly on top. This outlining, or building-up makes a pattern stand out more. The centre is finished with three deeper pink roses modelled from almond paste and arranged with maidenhair fern. The cake is circled with a pink ribbon to match the roses, the top edge and base of the cake neatened with a row

A cake decorated with an eight-point star pattern. The design on the cake is piped in royal icing.

of stars. This pattern is not difficult to execute – straight line patterns are always easier to achieve than curved designs. But one of the cardinal rules for success must always be remembered: never ice away or upwards; turn the cake when necessary so that the piping is always forwards and downwards.

To ice the cake board

On special occasion cakes the silver board should be covered with a layer of white or coloured icing to match the cake. This should be done when the last coat is put on the cake. Spread a thin layer of icing on the board round the cake to the edge of the board. Put the cake on a turntable and smooth the surface of the icing on the board with a palette knife, turning the cake at the same time. Clean the side edges of the board with a damp cloth before the icing has time to dry. When this smooth surface is quite set, decorate with trellis or braiding, and pipe dots, singly or in groups, around the edge of the board.

A cake with trellis work

This, as already explained, is fine parallel lines, crossing each other at right angles or diagonally. To fill an uneven space, begin with the centre line, and work parallel lines each side.

Braiding on a cake

This simply signifies a fine line worked in and out continuously, like a jig-saw pattern. There should be no straight lines, no lines touching each other, and no breaks in the continuity. Braiding over a thin layer of smooth icing gives a dainty finish to the cake board or to the surrounds of an eight-point star design.

An example of trellis work. These lines are worked at right angles to each other. The board is decorated with braiding over a smooth layer of icing.

A cake decorated with trellis work. The run-out cradle has a pastillage coverlet and stands on a pastillage plaque. An alternative design for the baby's cradle is also shown.

To decorate the sides of a royal iced cake

The most often used decoration on the sides of a cake is the hanging piped loop. After practice, it is quite easily achieved freehand. Touch a point on the top edge of the cake and allow the icing to come from the tube in a loop. Let the loop hang in mid-air until it is the correct length, and then attach it further along the cake simply by touching the top edge again. At first there will be some failures and some breakages, but with practice on a tin or a practice model, these errors will soon be eliminated.

A beginner can, if necessary, cut a template for the loops, by cutting a strip of paper the circumference of the cake and folding it according to the size and number of the loops required. Draw a loop on the folded paper, or fold in half and draw half the loop. Cut through the pencil line, and open out. Hold in position around the cake with an elastic band. For complete accuracy with the freehand method, judge the position of the loops according to the pattern on the top surface of the cake, and mark the positioning with dots of icing. Look at the drawings opposite to see the variety of ideas to be considered. Sometimes single loops are used, sometimes double loops. Most are elaborated with dots, either around or in between the loops.

But whatever pattern is attempted, it is always necessary to hold the tube away from the cake when making the loops, so that the icing falls into an even shape. The closer to the cake the tube is held, the harder the task becomes.

An alternative method is to tilt the cake on a turntable and work the loops $\frac{1}{8}$ inch ($\frac{1}{4}$ cm.) from the curved loop template, as if making a pattern on the top of the cake. Remove the template and over-pipe the loops.

Examples of designs suitable for the sides of a royal iced cake.

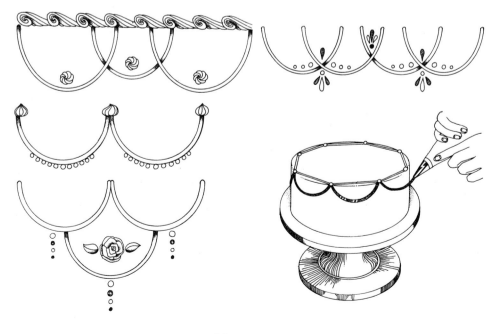

73

Baskets and lettering in royal icing

Some of the most beautiful and elaborate cakes can be achieved with royal icing. A basket with sugar pink roses is not difficult to make, the basket weaving tube is effective and does not require the practice that is needed for finer work. The only essential is patience, and an eye for perfection. The basket design is easy – in fact one of the easiest royal icing designs.

To make a basket of roses *Illustrated on page 62*
Never attempt this with anything other than a rich fruit cake, as much time may be needed to complete a basket, and the cake must last. The design is suitable for a birthday cake of any shape.

Cover the cake with almond paste and place on a silver cake board or drum 2 inches (5 cm.) larger than the diameter of the cake. Coat with one layer of white or coloured royal icing. Do not trouble with a perfect finish, as the basket work will cover the surface. When the icing is dry, make basket work stakes using royal icing and a No. 4 tube, working from the base upwards to the top of the cake. Always make an even number of stakes on both round and square cakes. To be sure about this, count the stakes when they are nearly completed, and decide whether two or three should be fitted in to make up the even number. The stakes should be absolutely upright and parallel, about $\frac{3}{4}$ inch ($1\frac{1}{2}$ cm) apart all around the cake. Leave the stakes to dry.

To work a square or oblong lid
Use a thin silver board the size and shape of the cake surface to represent the basket lid. Make stakes $\frac{3}{4}$ inch ($1\frac{1}{2}$ cm.) apart and parallel to each other straight on to the silver board. If the cake is oblong, cut the board in half and ice both halves with stakes to give the effect of a box lid opening at both sides from the centre.

The next day, when the stakes are dry, begin to form the weaving pattern. Using a fine ribbon tube (No. 23), start at the bottom of the basket, holding the hand sideways so that the icing can be tucked under the icing stake. Bring it from one stake over the next stake, and tuck it under the third, breaking off cleanly. Repeat all around the base of the cake. Continue, alternating each row until the whole of the side of the cake is covered in the weaving pattern. Weave square or oblong lids in the same way. Make a neat edge by piping a letter 'e' with a No. 1 tube continuously all around the base of the basket on the silver board, all around the top edge of the cake, and around the lid.

To work a round lid
Using a thin round silver board the same size as the top surface of the cake, make basket stakes as shown in the picture. Make the first stake across the centre of the board, and then cross it at right angles with the second. Divide into eighths with stakes reaching almost from the centre to the outer edge and continue halving

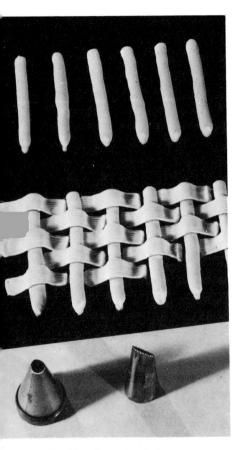

Working the basket design.

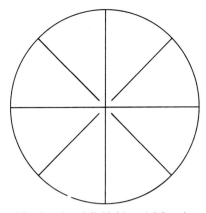

The silver board divided into eighths prior to working the basket design for the lid of a basket of roses cake.

Basket of roses cake.

each section until there is an even number of stakes $\frac{3}{4}$ inch ($1\frac{1}{2}$ cm.) apart all the way around the edge of the basket lid.

Begin the weaving on the outside edge first, again working over alternate stakes so that the weaving appears to be continuous. Near the centre, it will be necessary to work over two or three stakes, but the end of every stake must be covered. Make the weaving as neat as possible, although it will almost always end as a square in the middle. Any mistakes that are made can usually be camouflaged with a bow of ribbon.

To fill the basket with roses

Make roses following the directions given on page 39. Place the largest rose at the centre of one side of a square cake, or on the edge of a round cake. Using a knife or an icing bag cut to the size of a No. 1 tube, put a dab of icing on the rose, fixing in position with one of the curled back petals over the edge of the basket. Place the two largest of the remaining roses on each side of the first, and continue arranging, according to size and colour, until more than half the edge of the basket is covered. Place the lid in position, and adjust the roses so that the lid sits nicely in position. Arrange casually, pulling some roses out a little, pushing back others, and fitting in a few smaller roses where the board lid hinges on the cake at the back. Secure the lid in position with a little icing, making a continuous letter 'e' to form a hinge.

The number of roses needed will vary according to the size of the cake and the size of the flowers. Generally, about 12 roses should be made for an 8-inch (20-cm.) cake – any spare ones can always be saved for use in a later decoration. Any defects will be hidden, as before, by the ribbon bow across the top, which should tone in colour with the roses. A finishing touch can be given by inserting a sprig or two of pressed maidenhair fern or pressed asparagus fern between the roses.

A pleasant unexpected touch is added by writing a message of greeting on the cake before putting on the lid. This shows first as an extra surprise when the lid is removed, and the cake is about to be cut.

This basket work can also be made on a tin covered with waxed paper. Remove carefully and fill with sweets, or even strawberries when they are in season – this makes an unusual dessert.

A small basket for a cake top may be worked on a greased dish. Fill the dish with hot water and carefully remove from the dry icing.

Lettering

Lettering, whether simple or elaborate, adds to the pleasure given by an attractive, unusual cake. Simple script is naturally the easiest to achieve, but whatever writing is attempted, great care must be taken with accurate spacing. A perennial joke is made in the cartoons depicting a housewife icing 'happy birt' on a cake because she has no space to finish the word. To ice a long word like congratulations or anniversary across the middle of a cake, it is advisable to write it first in pencil on a piece of paper the same size as the cake, or else to try out the lettering on the practice board.

If script is used, begin with the middle letter of the greeting, and work both ways to complete it accurately. It is never necessary to write across the centre of a cake – indeed, this is the least interesting arrangement. Place a motif in one corner, and write the greeting circling, or half-circling the motif – for accuracy, make a space guide with a piece of paper.

Fold a sheet of paper in half and cut a quarter-circle, or whatever shape is needed, as in the drawing. Open out the paper and use on the cake as a guide to positioning the letters. Write or print through the hole in the paper, and then remove the guide. For two words, e.g. Christmas Greetings, turn the paper upside down for the second word, as in the drawings. This is effective, although even more unusual is the method of writing a word sideways. This looks particularly good with a single spray of flowers.

Several types of lettering are suitable for icing. One of the most attractive is serif lettering, shown opposite.

Practise by copying designs from magazines, greetings cards or newspapers, or books on Old English lettering. Stencils can also be bought and used as a guide for lettering. Spread stiff icing over them with a knife. When the stencil is removed, the letters remain. Always use firm royal icing for stencils, and not glacé icing.

Vary the style by using letters of uniform height, thickening the down stroke with a loop, designing a large first letter embellished with scroll work, and tiny flowers holding some of the smaller following letters. Fill in the outline of double letters with dots or run-in with soft sugar.

Experimentation is the keynote to good lettering. A greeting must be well done as bad lettering can spoil an otherwise perfect cake.

Examples of various types of lettering which can be used on a cake. A guide may be cut from a piece of paper for positioning lettering on the surface of a cake.

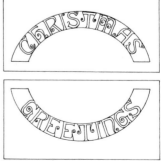

To pipe sugar flowers

To make icing flowers, keep practising on a practice board until perfect. This is the only way a good sugar flower can be achieved.

Most icing flowers are piped with a petal tube (Nos. 56–61). The nozzle is shaped in a long slit, wide at one end, and very narrow at the other.

Work on waxed paper after practice, or on small squares of waxed paper on an icing nail or a cork inserted in a small bottle. Use very stiff royal icing, coloured delicately according to the flower. Fix the square of waxed paper to the nail or cork with a dab of icing.

Snowdrops These are the simplest flowers to pipe, as a single petal is sometimes sufficient for one flower, or two or three at the most for an open bloom. The effect relies on good positioning. A spray of snowdrops makes a dainty and appealing decoration placed in one corner of a cake.

Use the petal tube with the hollow side uppermost and the wider end down on the board. Use well beaten white royal icing. Press out the icing, keeping the hand flat and moving round in a fan-like way. Each petal will resemble a tiny tooth. Pull off the tube with a quick downward movement. There will be a slight indentation in the centre of each petal, and a slightly raised curved edge.

To make a snowdrop with two petals, make one petal, and then pipe a second, over-wrapping the first. For a snowdrop with three petals, make two petals beside each other but with a little space between them, and then place a third on top and in the centre. Work on a practice board until the art has been mastered, and then begin working on the waxed paper. After 24 hours, store the petals in a box in a dry place, still on the waxed paper. When they are needed for use on a cake, pipe a small bulb of green icing and a hooked stem on to the cake, and place the sugar snowdrop in position with a little icing behind the flower to hold it in place. Using a little green colouring on an artist's brush, make a few tiny green lines on the petals. Pipe green lines on the cake to represent leaves.

Narcissi Again, work on a practice board at first, using white royal icing. Each flower has six petals placed adjoining each other in a circle. Touch the centre of the outer edge of each petal pulling out the icing, using the tube of icing or a pinhead to make a point as in the natural flower. Leave to dry, and then using a fine writing tube, make a spiral of icing to represent the trumpet. It is also possible, before adding the trumpet, to pipe one or three dots pulled up long in the centre of the flower, as the stamens and pistil.

When the completed flower is dry, paint the edge of the trumpet an orange colour, using food colouring and an artist's fine brush.

Daffodils Using yellow icing, follow the directions given for making narcissi. As each petal is made, touch the centre carefully,

A petal tube being used to pipe flowers.

Snowdrops

Narcissi

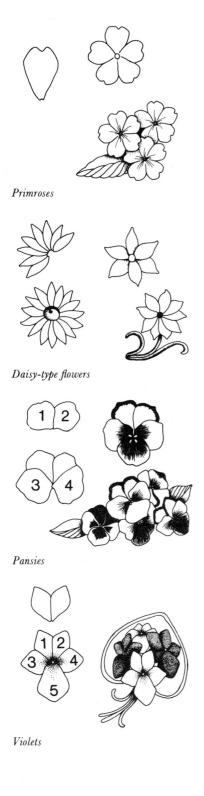

Primroses

Daisy-type flowers

Pansies

Violets

drawing it out in a longer point. A cocktail stick may be easier to use than the icing tube. Work the petals from left to right taking great care when icing the last petal not to spoil the first. Raise the tube a little to complete the last petal.

When the petals are dry, centre them with a long pistil, and make a yellow trumpet slightly deeper than for a narcissus. Finish the last time round with a wavy line to give the effect of a crimped edge. Vary the shade of the trumpet colour to deeper or paler yellow, or even to white. There are so many varieties of daffodils that it is almost impossible to go wrong with the shading.

Primroses Make five petals for each flower from a pale greeny-yellow icing. Move the hand up and down to form a heart shape, almost as if making two petals, and pull off sharply. When five petals have been completed, allow to dry and then finish the centre with a tiny green dot, adding a few streaks of green and yellow food colouring from the centre with an artist's brush. If possible, look at a natural flower or a good picture before adding these final details.

Daisy-type flowers Use almost any colour of icing: white for a field daisy or marguerite; mauve for a Michaelmas daisy; orange for a marigold; pink for pyrethrum, etc. Holding the petal tube at right angles to the waxed paper, with the wide part to the centre of the flower, press only very gently, and pull off the tube quickly. Make any number of petals, placing them closely in a circle, with no hole in the centre. For a daisy with wider petals, turn the tube the opposite way. Place a sugar-coated bulb in the centre, see page 80.

With practice, almost any flower can be represented, even a chrysanthemum. Use your ingenuity and imagination, as it is not possible to describe every type of flower.

Pansies Although these are difficult, wonderful effects can be achieved with patience. Practise on the board before attempting the flowers on waxed paper, and follow closely the order for icing each petal, given in the line drawing. Icing can always be scraped off a board back into the basin to be used again, but never scrape off waxed paper, as the grease may spoil the icing in the bowl.

Use two different colours for making a pansy, e.g., colour the two top petals yellow, and the rest mauve, or vice versa. Make petal one first, with two slightly over it. Then three and four, and finally number five, which is usually twice the size of the others. When making this last petal the first four petals should be upside down.

When the flower is quite dry, paint in the face with food colouring and a fine brush. Finish the centre with a dot of yellow. Again, look at a natural flower or picture to help perfect the colouring – two colours of icing in the one icing bag can give an unusual effect.

Violets Make these like pansies, using mauve or purple icing.

78

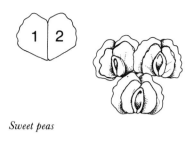

Sweet peas

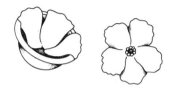

Forget-me-nots

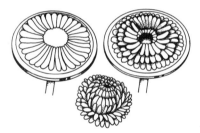

Petunias. The petals are first piped into a cup or cone shape made from heavy duty foil.

Chrysanthemums. These petals are first piped on to small squares of waxed paper secured to a flower nail.

Nasturtiums. These petals are first piped into a cup or cone shape as for a petunia.

Apple blossom

This is a hard colour to obtain, and sometimes, instead of the real deep dark-violet colour, paler violets have to be substituted. Centre with a green dot pulled out long with a tiny red dot on the end.

Sweet peas Using pink, white or mauve icing in varying shades, make two petals together with a slight frill at the edges. Make two smaller, fatter petals together, holding the tube at right angles to the first petals, and raising it in an upwards and downwards movement. Pull off quickly. This flower needs a lot of practice – it is difficult to describe, but with a little patience it is possible to teach oneself. With sweet peas, as with pansies, two colours in the icing bag are very effective.

Forget-me-nots, dog roses, etc. These can all be made following the basic directions. Five or six dots close together touching each other in a circle will form those small coloured flowers, with a centre dot of yellow. Larger flowers can be worked in blue or pink icing following the directions for a narcissus, but simply inserting a yellow dot in the flower centre.

Petunias The icing may be pink, purple, white or yellow. Make several cone or cup shapes from foil milk bottle tops or heavy duty foil. Pipe five petals in the cup shape with a petal tube making a frilly petal as for a sweet pea. Allow to dry a little then pipe yellow stamens and a green centre. Remove carefully from the foil cups when quite dry.

Chrysanthemums Using a flower nail with a small waxed paper circle secured with a little icing, make a shallow mould of icing on the paper with a small knife. With the petal tube make $\frac{1}{2}$-inch (1-cm.) long narrow pointed petals all around the outer edge of the mound. Make another row of shorter petals inside the first row and continue in this way until the whole mound is covered with petals. Make the petals in each row slightly shorter and bring them out and up until the centre petals are pulled right up. If necessary a yellow stamen may be piped in the centre. Use pink, white or bronze icing and a mixture of brown and yellow, or pink and darker pink in the same icing bag. Leave the chrysanthemums on the waxed paper to dry.

A chrysanthemum may also be fastened on a length of millinery wire dyed with food colouring to form a stem. Fix with stiff green royal icing after removing from the waxed paper.

Nasturtiums Use red or yellow icing, or have the two colours in the same bag. Pipe five frilly petals into foil cups as for a petunia. Make a division at the bottom of the petals with a skewer. (Refer to a real flower for this.) With food colouring, paint the centre of the flower green and paint in the dark lines coming from the centre.

Apple blossom Fill an icing bag, with a petal tube inserted, with pink icing in the thin side, and white in the thick side. Press out the icing into the bowl of pink icing until both pink and white are coming from the tube. Begin piping with the tube on its side,

79

the hollow side facing inwards, the thick end on the board and the thin end in the air. Press out a curled petal and, putting the tube inside the first petal, press out a second. Make five petals in all, to form a cup-shaped flower.

Although a small petal tube will make hawthorn, cherry and peach blossom, the bigger tube is more effective for apple blossom. Finish with a few long yellow dots in the flower centre. Arrange the blossoms on a twig made from a roll of almond paste coloured brown with food colouring and broken into different lengths. A few green leaves iced straight on to the branch with the blossom are very effective.

Sugar-centred flowers
Rub two or three drops of green, yellow or brown food colouring into a little castor or granulated sugar. Pipe various sized bulbs of icing on waxed paper, and before the icing is dry, sprinkle with the coloured sugar. Touch gently with the finger to make the sugar stick to the icing. Shake off any surplus sugar and leave to dry. Make daisy-type flowers and, while still wet, place one of

Royal iced cakes decorated with willow and an iced net butterfly.

these coloured centres in position, using the most suitable size to the flower.

In place of sugar it is possible to use strands of coloured sugar or hundreds and thousands.

Dahlias and sunflowers Pipe out two circles of petals on top of one another, making the inner ring with a hole in the centre. Fill the centre with a sugar-coated bulb.

Mimosa and willow Use yellow granulated sugar-coated bulbs to represent mimosa. Make longer shapes and coat with pale brown sugar to simulate willow catkins.

Use brown shades of sugar for depicting dogs, cats and birds on piped shapes.

Fluffy yellow chicks and ducklings make attractive decorations on an Easter cake. Make shapes with yellow icing and cover them, while still wet, with yellow castor sugar.

Tea roses Pipe the flowers on to the end of a cocktail stick, working from left to right with the thin end of the tube uppermost. Make the first petal over the top of the stick; the second over-lapping one-third of the first; and the third over-lapping one-third again, so that the three petals form a circle, always working from left to right. Continue making petals around the stick until the rose is the right size. Have ready some waxed paper, and pushing the pointed end of the cocktail stick through the paper, draw it through until the rose is left on the paper. This method ensures that the petals are held up.

Pipe tiny rosebuds on to a pin head and stick the pin in a pin cushion until the icing is dry. Make larger flowers on a skewer, and remove them by cutting the edge of the waxed paper, placing the skewer in the slit, and drawing it downwards, leaving behind the flower.

These flowers, too, are most effective piped with two colours of icing in the one icing bag.

These roses may be worked on green millinery wire to form stems; place them in a foam sponge to dry.

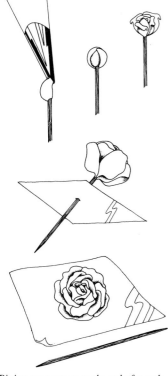

Piping tea roses on to the end of a cocktail stick. Before the icing has set transfer the rose to a piece of waxed paper and leave to dry.

Leaves

Green leaves to accompany the flowers can be made with a leaf tube, although generally this is only suitable for larger flowers. Using an icing bag only gives a better result for piping small leaves.

Fill the icing bag as usual, pressing the end flat between the thumb and finger. Cut the point in an inverted letter V like an arrow-head – for small leaves, cut only $\frac{1}{8}$ inch ($\frac{1}{4}$ cm.) from each side. Begin to pipe with the paper bag touching the waxed paper, and the end turning upwards. Press gently, and as the icing begins to come from each side of the V, slightly raise the bag, press out to the correct size, and pull off quickly to form a point at the end of the leaf. Alternatively make long, thin leaves to accompany

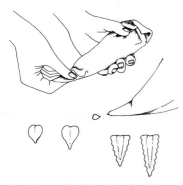

Preparing a filled icing bag for piping leaves by pressing the end flat between the thumb and finger and cutting the point in the shape of an inverted V.

81

An Easter egg cake made by baking the cake mixture in two pie dishes. The cakes are put together and covered with sugar paste and the design is piped in freehand.

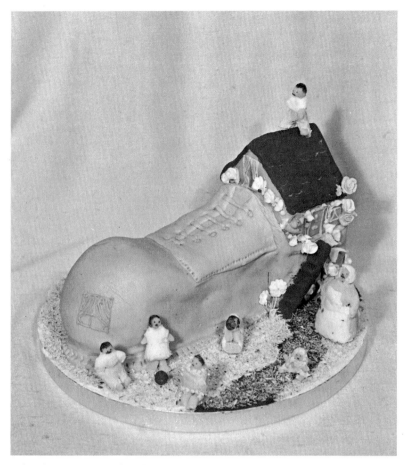

'The old woman who lived in a shoe' birthday cake covered with sugar paste and decorated with piped flowers. The cake mixture is baked in two loaf tins and cut to shape – one cake is placed in an upright position at the end of the other one.

A merry-go-round cake for a child's birthday covered with sugar paste and decorated with run-out horses.

daffodils, or a serrated fern-like leaf by moving the tube carefully backwards and forwards.

The best method of making a specific type of leaf is soon found by experimenting on the practice board. Make the leaves on waxed paper and store them for future use, or when proficient, pipe straight on to the cake.

White royal icing leaves can also be made – generally used for neatening and decorating wedding cakes. To give the effect of a vein to these leaves make a tiny cut in the centre of the V in the piping bag. For larger leaves cut a larger V shape, re-shaping the V cut with sharp scissors as the bag becomes worn. Re-press the end of the bag frequently between the thumb and finger.

Flowers made without a petal tube

Attractive flowers can be made using icing and an icing bag only. Press the end of the filled icing bag and cut an inverted V shape; follow the directions given on page 81 for piping out leaves. Make a series of petals working from the centre and pulling the bag outwards. These petals will be slightly more pointed than petals made with a tube, but a good result is possible with practice and for some flowers it is more realistic. Put a sugar-coated centre in place, or pipe in a round bulb using the icing bag with a small round hole cut in the end.

Forget-me-nots Make six dots in a circle on a square of waxed paper, using blue icing and the bag with the tip cut off. The dots should touch each other. Pipe a yellow dot, touching the blue dots, in the centre. Keep on the waxed paper until dry.

Delphinium and larkspur Make a number of forget-me-nots with yellow centres and leave to dry. Colour a length of millinery wire with green food colouring and pipe blue stars on the wire. While the icing is still wet, put the forget-me-not flowers all over the stars. If larger flowers are required, pipe blossoms with a small petal tube and use instead of the forget-me-nots to form delphiniums or to make larkspur spikes.

Fern Use millinery wire coloured green with food colouring. With an icing bag of green icing, pipe spikes all down the wire and on either side.

Water lilies Using an icing bag only cut in a V shape as for making leaves, make three or four petals in a circle on waxed paper, pulling upwards into long points instead of pulling out into a leaf shape. Touch the petal carefully, coaxing it to stand up, and even to curl inwards a little. Continue making petals outside the first three or four, until there are about 18 in all, piped close together. Finally add a few yellow dots in the centre and small green run-out leaves (see page 132).

Fern piped without a petal tube. Colour a length of millinery wire with green food colouring and pipe spikes all down the wire on each side.

Water lilies piped without a tube. These are made using an icing bag cut as for making leaves (see page 81).

Easter novelties and chocolate work

There is much more pleasure in making – and in giving – an Easter egg made and decorated at home, than in giving a silver-wrapped chocolate egg seen in dozens of shops all over the country. Some Easter novelties are easy to make. Some are more difficult. But with practice, and with patience, even the beginner can learn to make them all.

Decorated almonds

These are useful as Easter novelties, as they can be used to represent eggs. Buy some good quality sugared almonds in various colours. Using an icing bag only, fill with coloured royal icing and cut a very small hole. Make a line and dot flowers – daisies, dandelions, marguerites, Michaelmas daisies and even daffodils and hyacinths composed of dots, adding green stems and leaves (see page 81). When more proficient, short names can be piped on to the almonds.

This is good practice in the careful, fine work needed for more advanced designs and, with a little care and patience, delightful effects can be achieved.

When completed and dry, place each almond in a small paper case, then arrange altogether in a cellophane box.

Decorated Easter eggs

If Easter egg moulds are available, it is possible to make eggs with chocolate (see page 92), otherwise, buy some plain chocolate Easter eggs. Have ready a quantity of piped sugar flowers. Try out arrangements of flowers on the practice board first to perfect balance and colour and to ensure adequate space is left to pipe the child's name if necessary.

Flowers and names piped on to sugared almonds. These make useful Easter novelties.

A chocolate Easter egg decorated with piped flowers. The butterfly and orchid are made from pastillage.

A Wendy house cake made by baking the cake mixture in two round cake tins. The cakes are put one on top of each other and covered with sugar paste.

A crinoline lady cake. The cake mixture is baked in a basin and decorated with royal icing using a petal tube, and piped flowers (see page 108).

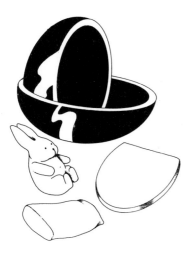

Scratch the surface of the chocolate egg with a sharp, pointed tool – e.g. a long needle – put on a dot of icing, and fix the flower before the icing has time to dry. When the arrangement is complete, pipe in green stems. An icing bow can be made, using the serrated ribbon tube. If a large egg is being decorated, make the bow on waxed paper and leave to dry before putting in place. Small almond paste roses are also suitable for decorating Easter eggs; cut off some of the base of the roses as soon as they are made, so that they are not too long to place on the egg.

Neaten the join of the egg with a row of icing shells or scrolls, or tie a piece of ribbon, silver braid or lace around the egg. The final result should be one of prettiness and daintiness.

Place the finished egg in the centre of a square of cellophane. Draw up to the top and fasten with an elastic band. If the egg has no ribbon, tie the cellophane with a ribbon bow. The whole effect is expensive and professional.

Rabbits
Use a small egg for the rabbit head and a larger one for the body. Pipe the face on the smaller egg, complete with ears and whiskers. White dots of royal icing with chocolate centres make the eyes. Use icing to fix the small egg in a suitable position on the larger egg, and pipe icing lines or use rolls of almond paste for front and back legs. Place in a box on a bed of green paper straw, or arrange on green shredded coconut.

Hens and chickens
Roll out some red or yellow pastillage thinly, and cut out a red cock's comb or a small yellow crest, and place in position on the egg, fixing it with royal icing. Make the beak in the same way, and pipe in the eyes. When firm, wrap in cellophane and pack in a box.

Easter egg cradle
Using two halves of a hollow Easter egg, place the smaller end of one half into the larger end of the other half, tilting slightly to form a cradle with a canopy. Fasten in position with royal icing. Roll out natural-coloured almond paste or sugar paste to form a coverlet; make a cradle pillow, and mould a small figure for the baby or rabbit. Assemble the whole cradle, and finally pipe lines of trellis and lace work on the coverlet.

An Easter egg cradle. The cradle is made from two halves of a hollow Easter egg. The coverlet and figures are moulded from natural-coloured almond paste and the pattern is piped in royal icing.

Chocolate work

Always carry out chocolate work in a medium temperature. Too hot a temperature prevents chocolate from setting, and too cold a temperature will make it set too quickly and may also cause it to set dull instead of shiny.

To temper chocolate

For large-scale production of chocolate work it is necessary to temper the chocolate. For best results the use of a thermometer is recommended.

Break up plain chocolate and melt it in a double saucepan with hot, not boiling, water in the outer pan. Melt the chocolate to 100–115°F. (38–46°C.). Stir well, remove the pan of chocolate to a pan of cold water and cool to 80–82°F. (27–28°C.), stirring thoroughly. Replace the pan of chocolate on the hot water and reheat to 88–90°F. (31–32°C.), stirring all the time. The chocolate is now ready for use.

For milk chocolate use 2°F. (1°C.) lower temperature in each case.

For cake coating use a good brand of covering chocolate broken into small pieces and put into a double saucepan or a basin covered with a saucer. Allow some water to come almost to the boil in the bottom half of the double saucepan and place the top half, or a covered basin in position on the almost boiling water. Do not allow the water to boil or the chocolate will become lumpy. Remove immediately from the heat and leave to stand for a while. When the water is cool, the chocolate will be ready.

When the chocolate has had time to melt, remove from the water and beat with a wooden spoon without letting any water or steam get into the chocolate. Have the cake ready on a plate with a doily and pour the chocolate on to the centre of the cake, coaxing it over the top surface just to the edge, in the same way as a glacé icing. Leave undisturbed to set. When set, pipe with a simple pattern. Add two drops of glycerine or a little stock syrup (see page 11) to chocolate for piping.

Chocolate boxes

While the chocolate is melting, place a piece of waxed paper on a flat surface (use the wrapping from a breakfast cereal packet or a sliced loaf). When the chocolate is melted, beat and pour it on to the waxed paper. Spread evenly with a knife and make a neat, straight edge. Leave to set a little, and as soon as the chocolate is beginning to darken, cut into 2-inch (5-cm.) squares with a knife. Leave to become quite hard.

Meanwhile, prepare pink butter cream, squares of Madeira or genoese sponge cake, slightly smaller than the chocolate squares. Using the cream or some jam, fix four squares of chocolate, one to each side of the cake squares, using as the outside, the chocolate that was next to the waxed paper. Pipe a large butter cream rosette in the top and arrange a lid of chocolate at an angle.

Chocolate torton

Melt the chocolate as before (use about 4 oz. (100 g.) chocolate to cover a 7-inch (19-cm.) cake; a further 2 oz. (50 g.) for the sides).

A gâteau topped with chocolate crème au beurre and decorated with chocolate triangles.

Chocolate boxes.

89

A village of models made from sugar paste and royal icing.

A birthday cake decorated with trellis panels in royal icing.

A christening cake decorated with run-out letters and moulded roses. The cradle is made from run-out pieces; the coverlet may be made from sugar paste or pastillage.
A royal iced cake showing how an effective decoration can be made using a serrated scraper. Standing lace pieces are placed around the edges and the braiding is repeated on the edge of the board (see page 72). Small cakes covered with boiled fondant icing and decorated with small piped flowers.

Meanwhile, cut a circle of waxed paper the size of the outside of the bottom of the tin in which the cake – a chocolate mixture or a Madeira – has been baked. Also cut a strip of waxed paper the correct size to go around the cake, with a little extra length in case of breakages. When the chocolate is ready, pour on to both pieces of waxed paper, coaxing it over to the edge of the circle, and spreading it the length of the strip.

When the chocolate begins to darken, cut through the centre of the circle, and diagonally in eight or twelve positions to make triangles a suitable size for the top of the cake. Cut the strips into pieces ½ inch (1 cm.) wide. Leave to set. Meanwhile, make 4–6 oz. (100–175 g.) butter cream, coloured and flavoured with cocoa powder or instant coffee. Spread over the top of the cake evenly and, if liked, put in a filling.

Spread jam or cream around the sides of the cake, and carefully lift the ½-inch (1-cm.) chocolate strips and arrange them around the cake, in each case using the side that has been next to the waxed paper as the outside. Pipe eight or 12 stars on top of the cake at even places – pipe these rather tall to raise the chocolate triangles. Set the triangles at a slant on the stars, again with the smooth side uppermost, and with the points to the centre, like an electric fan. Finally, pipe a scroll of butter cream on each triangle and a rosette in the centre of the cake. Before serving, tie a piece of gilt cord in a bow around the cake to hold the chocolate strips in place. If preferred, chocolate vermicelli can be used on the side of the cake instead of the chocolate strips.

For a games party, decorate a cake as shown opposite. Follow the method above for making the chocolate shapes, using metal cutters or hand-cut paper templates for the heart, diamond, spade and club designs.

To pipe chocolate

Draw the shapes required – wheels, snowflakes, hearts, etc. – on greaseproof paper, and then cover with thin waxed paper. Melt the chocolate and beat well, adding at the most 2–3 drops of glycerine or 1 teaspoon stock syrup (see page 11) to 4 oz. (100 g.) chocolate. Beat again, cool a little, and put into a greaseproof paper icing bag as for royal icing. Pipe on to the waxed paper, following the sketches on the greaseproof paper underneath. As well as simple shapes, scrolls in batches, chocolate hearts, a music clef and notes, swans' heads to top cream bodies on a fruit gâteau can be piped out. When set, remove these shapes from the waxed paper and store until required. A simple design need not always be made beforehand, but can be piped straight on to a chocolate-coated cake.

Chocolate Easter eggs

Special moulds must be bought to make chocolate eggs. When

Chocolate torton. The pieces of chocolate are cut when almost set, as for chocolate boxes.

Games cake. The shapes are cut when almost set, as for chocolate boxes.

not in use, always keep them in a paper bag in an airtight tin to protect them from the atmosphere; before using, polish up the inside of the mould by rubbing it with a piece of cotton wool. If necessary, for easy removal of the chocolate egg shape, grease the moulds slightly with castor oil, rubbing it well to remove any surplus. Avoid making finger-marks on the inside of the mould as these will show on the chocolate egg.

Pour the melted chocolate into the egg mould and run it around to cover the entire inside surface to the edges. Pour out the surplus chocolate before it can begin to set. Put into a cold place immediately. Never put into a refrigerator, as the intense cold will shrink the chocolate too quickly. When the chocolate has set it will have shrunk slightly. Pare the edge with a palette knife and, using the same knife, remove the chocolate carefully from the mould – sometimes it can be shaken out. Take care not to break the egg shape.

To fix the two halves of an egg together, heat water to almost boiling point in an aluminium saucepan, and carefully and quickly brush the edge of the egg across the outside of the warm pan. Just as quickly, put the two egg halves together. The melted chocolate should seal to make a complete egg. This needs practice, but it is a very practical way of doing the job.

If moulds are available, animals can also be made in this way.

Decorated chocolate Easter eggs placed on a cake topped with butter cream marked with a serrated scraper.

A birthday cake in royal icing with lace pieces standing off the edge, and autumn leaves.
A garden design cake.

A heart-shaped cake for an engagement party, decorated with lace pieces standing off the edge. An attractive edging for a square cake.

Painted pastillage plaques for decorating Christmas cakes.

The top of a Christmas cake decorated with a whole run-out. The raised base collar and top are decorated with royal icing icicles; the figures are standing run-outs and the snow is made from rock sugar (see page 164).

Pastillage Christmas cards showing these can be opened.

Home-made chocolates

Chocolate centres can be made from almond paste cut into shapes, very stiff royal icing rolled into balls, or pieces of crystallised fruits. Lower one centre at a time into melted chocolate using a dipping fork. Remove and shake off the surplus chocolate drawing it across the side of the pan. Place the chocolate on waxed paper or a wire rack to set. Arrange in individual papers in a fancy box.

It is necessary to temper the chocolate first if any quantity is required or if they are to be kept any length of time. If tempering is omitted the chocolate sets slowly and may be dull and have a patchy appearance.

Florentines

IMPERIAL/METRIC

¼ pint/1½ dl. single cream
3 oz./75 g. castor sugar
3 oz./75 g. candied orange peel
4 oz./100 g. blanched almonds
1 oz./25 g. glacé cherries
1 teaspoon plain flour
½ oz./15 g. butter
2 oz./50 g. plain chocolate

Oven temperature: moderately hot (375°F., 190°C., Gas Mark 5)
Makes: about 45
Cooking time: about 8 minutes

Put the cream and sugar in a heavy-bottomed saucepan and heat slowly until the sugar has dissolved. Meanwhile cut the orange peel and almonds into strips and chop the cherries. Add to the cream mixture together with the flour and butter. Remove from the heat and mix thoroughly. Place small heaps of the mixture well apart on greased and floured baking trays. Flatten each heap slightly with a knife. Bake in a moderately hot oven for about 8 minutes, until golden brown. Remove from the trays at once and cool on a wire rack. When cold, spread the bottom of the biscuits with melted chocolate (melted in the top of a double saucepan or a bowl over a pan of hot water) and draw a serrated scraper over to make a zig-zag pattern.

Chocolate cups

IMPERIAL/METRIC

8 oz./225 g. chocolate
2 oz./50 g. butter
2 oz./50 g. icing sugar
4 oz./100 g. cake or soft
  breadcrumbs
2 oz./50 g. glacé cherries,
  chopped
2–3 tablespoons cocoa powder
2–3 tablespoons apricot jam
few drops vanilla or rum essence

Makes: about 9 chocolate cups

Melt the chocolate slowly in a basin placed over a pan of hot, not boiling, water. Keep the basin covered to avoid steam getting into the chocolate. Pour some of the melted chocolate into an individual foil or paper baking case and swirl it around until the inside of the case is coated with chocolate. Pour the surplus chocolate back into the basin. Repeat until all the chocolate has been used.

Cream the butter and icing sugar together. Mix in the crumbs, cherries, cocoa powder and sufficient apricot jam to make a moist mixture. Flavour to taste with essence. Spoon the mixture into the chocolate cases and leave in a cool place until firm. Just before serving, peel away the cases and dredge the tops with icing sugar.

Party biscuits and cakes

As a change from the concentration needed to ice an elaborate cake, ice novelty biscuits for a children's party or a Valentine's Day tea. Design beautiful old-fashioned ladies in crinoline skirts, or chocolate sponge engines and pop-eyed gingerbread men to delight the children.

Feather-iced biscuits

Use plain bought tea biscuits or make Shrewsbury biscuits (see page 185) cut into 3- or 4-inch (7½- or 10-cm.) rounds. When baked and cold, ice with white or pale coloured glacé icing. Have ready an icing bag of glacé icing flavoured and coloured with cocoa powder or food colouring. While the glacé icing is still wet, pipe straight lines ½ inch (1 cm.) apart across the biscuit, and while both the surface and piping are still wet, draw a knife at right angles through the piping lines, again at intervals of ½ inch (1 cm.) to produce a loop effect.

Ice and pipe exactly the same design on a second biscuit, but draw the knife across in lines 1 inch (2½ cm.) apart, turn the biscuit around and draw the knife back in lines again 1 inch (2½ cm.) apart, between the previous cuts, making a feather pattern.

On another biscuit, pipe circles, beginning with a small circle in the centre and encircling it with larger circles, each one ½ inch (1 cm.) outside the other. Draw a knife from the centre outwards in eight positions, as if cutting a cake. This produces a spider's web effect. Alternatively, draw the knife from the outside to the middle in the same eight positions, or draw the knife outwards in quarters, and divide each quarter by drawing the knife inwards, or vice versa. These two patterns produce an attractive flower design.

As another, completely different design, pipe diametrical lines dividing the biscuit into eight parts, and draw the knife round and round in a circular movement. This gives a pinwheel effect.

Vary the icing colours and try out different patterns. Always serve these biscuits the same day they are iced while they are crisp.

The same patterns may be used for icing cakes.

Ladies' fingers

Buy a packet of sponge finger biscuits or make sponge finger cakes. Place royal icing in an icing bag with a No. 1 tube inserted; pipe a line around the edge of the biscuit. Cover the surface of the biscuit inside the piped area with soft royal icing. Bring the icing just to the line but do not break or the icing will flow over the edge.

When set, using the icing bag only, pipe a wavy trail of green royal icing the length of each biscuit to represent a stem. When completed, cut the end of the bag to a v-shaped point to make tiny leaves shooting at intervals from the green trail. At the top of

Feather-iced biscuits showing several patterns.

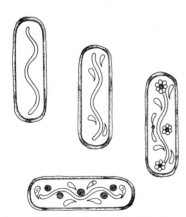

Sponge finger biscuits covered with soft royal icing and piped with designs using a No. 1 tube.

A pastillage squirrel plaque, and greetings card with a dog. This is raised royal icing known as shaggy work (see page 128). The picture shows the correct way to hold an icing bag.

A square wedding cake decorated in a Wedgwood design (see page 125).

each trail add a circle of white or bright coloured dots in royal icing, centred with a yellow dot, to form a flower. Alternatively, at intervals on the stem add any red almond paste berries left over from making holly.

Valentine biscuits *Illustrated on page 18*

Roll out the Shrewsbury biscuit dough (see page 185) to about ⅛ inch (¼ cm.) in thickness. Cut into heart shapes with a metal cutter or by folding a piece of paper in half, drawing on it half of a heart shape, cutting through the pencil line, and opening out a heart-shaped paper guide. Lay this on the rolled out biscuit dough and cut round with a knife.

Place the shapes on a greased baking tray and cook in a moderate oven (350°F., 180°C., Gas Mark 4) until pale brown, turning the baking trays around to bake the biscuits evenly. Cool on a wire tray.

If liked, make a few biscuits about 6 inches (15 cm.) in diameter to give plenty of scope for piping on the designs.

The ways of decorating Valentine biscuits are endless – sprays of piped flowers and raised lace patterns are just two ideas out of many. When the biscuits are cool, ice a line about ¼ inch (½ cm.) in from the edge, all around the edge of the biscuit, using white royal icing and a No. 1 tube. Fill the centre with white or pale coloured glacé icing, or royal icing thinned down with a little water or egg white. On the outside of the piped line, when the centre is dry, pipe a lace edge to the biscuit, consisting of dots: two dots together, topped with a third dot on the outside, at intervals around the edge, or pyramids of dots, starting with three, then two, and then one. Alternate different ideas of lacy points, scallops and fringes, and complete with flower arrangements and letters. See page 112 for more advanced, intricate lace work designs.

Animal biscuits

Again using the Shrewsbury biscuit dough, cut out animal or figure shapes with cutters, or make a paper pattern and cut out with a knife, as the heart-shape biscuits were made. Suitable animal shapes can often be cut from newspaper advertisements or tracings taken from children's picture books. Pipe around the edge of the baked biscuit and fill the centre with glacé or thinned royal icing.

When dry, pipe in the face, and outline any clothing.

Gingerbread men

These party biscuits are quick and easy to make, as very little detail is required.

Use a ginger biscuit or gingerbread pastry recipe (see page 185). Roll a ball for the head about the size of a thimble, and another

These designs shown on Valentine cakes could also be worked on heart-shaped biscuits.

Examples of designs suitable for piping on to Valentine biscuits. A heart shape may be cut from a piece of paper, as shown, to use as a guide for cutting out the biscuit shapes.

A gingerbread house. The pieces for the house may be cut from rolled out ginger biscuit or ginger pastry mixture.

about the size of an egg for the body. Make two rolls for the legs and two for the arms. Flatten out in position on a greased baking tray, placing the head, arms and legs against the body. Leave plenty of room between the figures, as the mixture will spread. Bake, and loosen carefully with a palette knife or fish slice. When partly cooled, transfer to a wire rack. When quite cold, pipe the face, and perhaps add a hat and buttons.

Gingerbread donkeys can be made using the same method.

Gingerbread house

Make a pattern for a square house, or cut up a suitable size cardboard box and use in the same way. Use four pieces for walls, two for the roof, and perhaps two further pieces to represent a fence and a gate. Grease the back of the cardboard, lay it on rolled out ginger biscuit or ginger pastry mixture and cut to shape. Place the pieces on a baking tray and bake in a moderate oven (350°F., 180°C., Gas Mark 4) for about 10 minutes, until lightly browned. Remove carefully on to a wire rack to cool.

When quite cold, fix the house together, using royal icing on the inside to join the pieces. Prop with jars until the icing is quite firm, and then pipe in royal icing doors and windows. Stand the house on a silver board covered with green coconut or rough green icing, to represent grass. Add the fence and gate and a few piped flowers. Chocolate drops may be used to tile the roof, and a gingerbread man put in the garden. There is no end to the scope, and the fun to be had making this novelty.

Biscuit clocks

Pipe a circle around the edge of baked Shrewsbury biscuits (see page 185). Cover the centre with glacé icing. When dry, pipe on the numbers and the clock hands. These can be iced straight on to the biscuit surface, but the piping does not always stick well.

Funny face biscuits

Pipe eyes, nose and mouth in coloured icing on to baked pink-iced Shrewsbury biscuits (see page 185). The funnier the faces, the more amusing the result, and the more popular the biscuits will be with children.

To ice with a stencil

Children's stencil painting kits are often used for quick letter and picture decorations on a cake. Use a surface of royal icing or sugar paste, as the stiff parchment paper may spoil a soft surface of glacé icing.

Find a suitable pattern, place the stencil in position on the cake, and spread quickly with a stiff royal or fudge icing. Remove the stencil carefully, leaving behind the pattern. Add any necessary outlining or details in royal icing.

Examples of designs which can be piped on to biscuits. Pipe a circle around the outside edge of the biscuit and then cover the centre with glacé icing.

A round wedding cake, decorated in a Wedgwood design, with scalloped collars (see page 125).

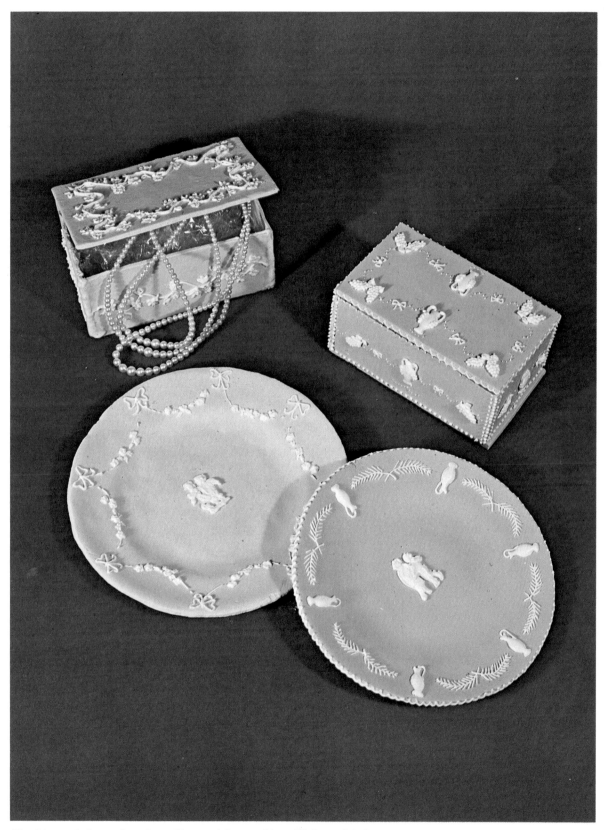

Novelties made from coloured pastillage and decorated in a Wedgwood design (see page 124).

Two chocolate Swiss rolls modelled into an engine cake for a child's birthday cake.

A child's birthday cake made from a Swiss roll and squares of cake covered with coloured sugar paste.

Children's party cakes

Large letter or number stencils can be used to good effect on small, square cakes to represent building bricks, chocolate Swiss rolls modelled into an engine and spelling bricks at a party for young children.

Cover square pieces of cake with different coloured sugar paste. With the finger, rub cornflour gently across the surface for a smooth finish. Using large stencil letters and numbers, spread royal icing across, allowing one side to dry before making a second letter on another side. Alternatively, the numbers can be piped on to the cakes.

For variety, stencil bold simple scenes: ducks or chickens following each other, houses, or a figure with balloons.

Bought plain biscuits, or home-made ones, iced with run-out royal icing (see page 132) can be stencilled easily, and make pretty place names for a children's party. For savouries, stencil cream cheese on to plain biscuits, making a name, a picture, or any simple design.

A variation on these methods is to dredge icing sugar over a stencil. Dredge the word lemon across a lemon cake, orange on an orange cake and so on, or place a doily on a cake and dredge over with icing sugar for a quick decoration on a sponge or sandwich cake. Lift off the doily leaving behind the sugar pattern.

To ice with butter cream

Butter cream is an excellent icing for piping quick designs. It is a soft icing which can be flavoured and coloured. Follow the recipe given on page 17, but only begin piping with butter cream when well practised with royal icing. Make a slightly larger greaseproof bag, using paper about 8 inches (20 cm.) by 12 inches (30 cm.), cut diagonally. Form the bag and cut off the end of the bag, and insert a No. 5 or 8 star tube, according to the work.

To ice a bar cake

Use an oblong Madeira or light fruit cake mixture baked in a loaf tin. Coat the sides with jam or butter cream and chopped nuts or toasted coconut. Using the star tube and a natural coloured butter cream, pipe a line down each of the long edges on the top of the cake, and a line down the centre. Colour the remaining butter cream pink, and again using the star tube, work a line of close zig-zagging between the two lines of natural coloured cream. This should cover the entire top surface of the cake. Finally, add a little cocoa powder to the pink cream and pipe stars $\frac{1}{2}$ inch (1 cm.) apart along the top of the central line. Make these stars by holding the star tube near the work and pressing out the icing until the star is the right size. Stop pressing and pull off quickly but carefully. Try this out first on a practice board.

Chocolate hearts cake

Coat the sides of a sandwich cake or genoese sponge with cream and chopped nuts. Fill a paper icing bag with red or green piping jelly (this can be bought, but if unobtainable, use sieved apricot jam, either natural coloured, or with red or green food colouring added). Pipe lines of jelly across the cake diagonally, dividing the surface into eight parts. Using the star tube, pipe natural coloured cream zig-zags into each section, beginning in the centre and working to the outside, making the lines gradually longer to cover the whole of each section. To give variety, colour may be used in alternate sections. Decorate the top with piped chocolate hearts (see page 92), cherries or piped flowers.

To make a pattern with a serrated scraper

Use this only on the firmer cakes – Madeira or a Victoria sandwich. Spread the top and sides with hot apricot glaze, and when set and cold, cover the surface as smoothly as possible with a thin layer of butter cream. Leave to set in a refrigerator or any cool place. When set, spread more thickly with butter cream, then use the scraper to make a pattern on the top and around the sides. Pipe zig-zag lines from the centre of the cake in pale pink, green or orange butter cream and finish each end with a large star. Have ready some piped chocolate shapes and arrange around the edge of the cake, adding piped flowers to tone with the colour of the cream. Neaten the lower edge, as well as the top edge, with a scroll, shell or star; practise the scrolls on a board first, holding the tube in the same way as for a star, and moving it round into a sideways question mark line. Pull off quickly so that the scroll thins out to nothing, and fit the second scroll on the tail of the first. A shell is made as if making a star, but bring the tube forward and straight down, pulling off quickly, pressing out only the necessary amount of icing for the shell.

See the picture on page 23 for other designs using butter cream.

A cake piped with butter cream and decorated with chocolate hearts. Right, a cake topped with butter cream and a pattern made with a serrated scraper.

A cake coated with blue icing and decorated with run-out swans pulling a sleigh.

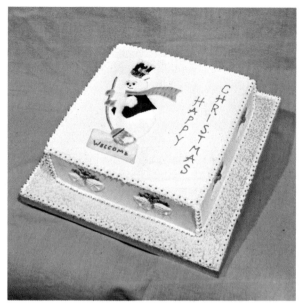

A Christmas cake decorated neat lettering, a painted design and bells on the sides.

A birthday cake decorated with pink run-out elephants.

A birthday cake for a music enthusiast showing a disc and composers' names on plaques placed on the top edge of the cake.

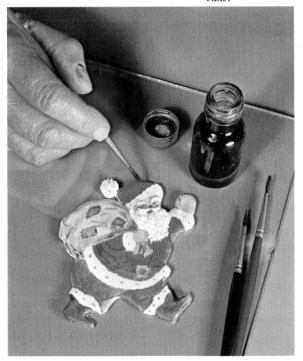

A run-out of Father Christmas. The final touches being put on his cap with food colouring.

A model of a church made from a cake cut to shape and covered with sugar paste. The trellis is worked with royal icing.

To make a crinoline lady cake

This is a quick decoration that looks very attractive and intricate. Bake a Madeira cake mixture in an ovenproof basin, using 6 oz. (175 g.) flour etc. to a 1½-pint (1-litre) basin. Grease the basin well and put two strips of paper in the base and up the sides. Bake the mixture for about 1¼ hours in a moderate oven (350°F., 180°C., Gas Mark 4), as the basin is thick and the cake deep. Remove the cake from the basin with the paper strips and cool on a wire rack. Cut the top level, coat the sides with apricot glaze if liked, and place upside down on a silver board. Have ready a china model head.

Make up butter cream using 4 oz. (100 g.) margarine and 4 oz. (100 g.) sifted icing sugar. Beat well. Spread the front of the cake smoothly to represent the apron front, and mark in pleats with a knife. Avoid pulling up crumbs from the cake (this does not happen if apricot glaze has been used). With a star tube and a paper icing bag rather larger than usual as a lot of cream will be needed, make four loops of natural coloured butter cream to join each side of the apron, representing panniers. Fill in the loops with natural coloured stars, fitted in close together. Keeping back enough natural coloured cream for bows and decoration, colour the remainder to match the china head. Using the coloured cream, pipe stars close together covering the entire remainder of the cake right down to the board.

To finish, add food colouring to the reserved butter cream and using a No. 1 tube, pipe decorations of dots and hanging loops on the apron front, and add three bows at the top of the loops or panniers. Place the china doll's head in position and neaten the waistline with some cream. Leave in a cool place to set.

This basic design can be varied in several ways. The cake can be covered with almond paste and royal icing and decorated with frills piped with a petal tube as in the picture on page 87. If covering the cake with royal icing use a rich fruit cake mixture instead of a Madeira cake mixture.

When baking the mixture for a crinoline lady cake, place two strips of grease-proof paper in the base and up the sides of the ovenproof bowl so that the baked mixture can be lifted out easily. The decoration may be piped with a star tube and butter cream, or with a petal tube and royal icing as shown in the drawing.

Trellis work and lace piping work

This is perhaps the most delicate of all icing work, and yet when it is expertly carried out, it is remarkable how easily the pieces can be handled without breaking.

As a beginning, practise making dome or boat-shaped pieces of simple icing lace work – similar to a trellis – over inverted patty tins, small egg poacher pans, or boat-shaped tins. Later, use a cream horn tin, a napkin ring or the side of a cocoa tin.

Before beginning to work, grease the outside of the mould thoroughly with lard or cooking fat. Grease the edges particularly well. Using a No. 1 tube in an icing bag and well beaten royal icing, pipe a single line of icing around the base of the mould, over the grease, to give strength and to act as a guiding line. Make a second line right over the centre of the mould, from the guiding line at one side to the guiding line at the other side, dividing the mould in half. Continue making lines a $\frac{1}{4}$ inch ($\frac{1}{2}$ cm.) apart, parallel to the central line, right across the mould.

When these lines are completed, begin making lines across to form a trellis, either at right angles, to give small squares, or at an angle of 45°, to give a diamond pattern. If extra strength is needed, add a third row of lines, varying the pattern by cutting through the squares or diamonds already made. Finally, again to give added strength, make a thicker rim around the edge of the lace work, with the same tube, and pipe a whipped line using a series of e-shaped twists. Put the worked moulds in a dry, warm place for several days before removing the set icing.

If any mistakes occur, and the icing is scraped off the mould, it will be necessary to grease the mould again. The discarded icing must on no account be put back into the bowl, as the grease in it would spoil the clean, unused icing.

When the icing is quite dry, place the mould in the left hand (over a cloth on the hand if too hot), with the icing side down against the cloth on the hand, supporting it gently by cupping the fingers lightly round the mould. Now carefully pour hot water from the spout of a good pouring kettle, until it nearly fills the mould. The heat will melt the fat, a tiny tinkling noise will be heard and, with care, the mould full of water can be lifted from the icing, leaving the rounded trellis in the hand. Carefully lift by the edge, and place in a box on a bed of cotton wool.

These domes can be used on formal, highly decorative cakes, particularly wedding cakes, or even more effectively, by placing something under the raised trellis cage: a sprig of almond paste holly on a Christmas cake, small piped flowers, or a silver shoe.

As a change from the trellis effect, make a lace pattern piping a design from the letters 's', 'c' and 'x'. As before, the mould must first be greased on the outside, and a single line of icing piped around the edge of the mould, using a No. 1 tube.

This time, fill the centre with these three letters, all touching each other, filling the whole surface of the mould and joining the

Piping a lace work pattern over inverted patty tins.

A trellis design and a raised trellis cage with roses underneath.

A run-out collar on a cake decorated with a three-dimensional design.

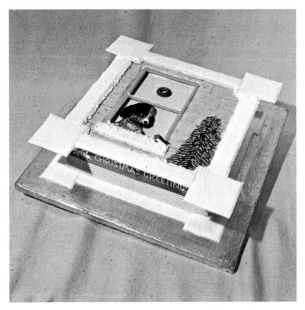

A Christmas cake decorated with a neat collar and a scene showing a dog in the window.

A cake decorated with a three-dimensional winter scene. The collar is decorated with lace work leaves.

A three-dimensional cake decorated with a collar. A serrated scraper has been used to make the neat sides.

An attractively designed collar on a cake decorated with a winter scene.

A cake decorated with a scalloped collar and a Christmas scene.

An attractive Christmas cake decorated with an unusual run-out collar.

A Christmas cake decorated with a figure of a shepherd boy.

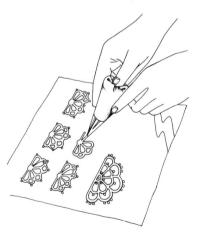

Two designs suitable for flat lace and trellis work piping.

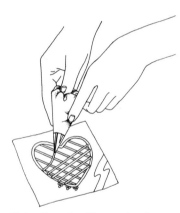

Piping lines of trellis to make a heart-shaped design.

Piping out small lace pieces to decorate the top edge of an iced cake.

edge. Letters must all be made touching each other. If there are any pieces not joined, the icing lace will break when it is taken from the mould. If any small spaces are found between the letters when the icing is completed, a small dot can be used to make the join. Finally, strengthen with a whipped edge or a line of the letter 'e'. Remove from the mould with hot water as before and store in a warm dry place, in a box lined with cotton wool.

Keep a store of these filigree domes, and use them on the centre of a glacé iced cake for quick effect. Do not keep too long on the glacé icing, as the dampness tends to make the dome collapse if the cake is kept for several hours or overnight. It is preferable to put the decoration on glacé icing only just before serving, and to use the cake the same day.

Flat lace work piping

Begin by making a trellis which is a series of lines crossing each other at right angles or diagonally; work on waxed paper if the trellis is to be lifted and placed on the cake. Any shape may be followed and if working an uneven shape, begin in the centre and work to the sides so that the lines can be kept straight and even.

The drawing shows two shapes for flat lace work piping. Draw out these (or other) shapes on a firm piece of paper. Fasten them down on a practice board, or the back of a plate or a piece of glass, with a dot of icing, or use a piece of clear adhesive tape. Cover the shape with waxed paper and secure it at the corners. It is better to cover each shape with its own piece of waxed paper to avoid possible breakages at a later stage.

Using a No. 1 tube and white or coloured icing, pipe a fine line around the edge of the design. Then work in the trellis – work a line across the middle then work parallel lines each side, then lines again at right angles, beginning with the middle line. Decorate the edge with small dots or picot (three or six dots together); if liked, work three dots near together, miss an $\frac{1}{8}$ inch ($\frac{1}{4}$ cm.) and continue with three more dots. If working round a pattern, arrange the dots so that the number of dots fits the pattern. Place one dot between the first two, but out a little, and one between the next two dots and a last dot between the two just made, to form a lace edging. The dots of icing should touch each other, otherwise they will fall off when the lace motif is lifted from the waxed paper.

Leave the lace in a warm room overnight, to become quite dry. The next day, carefully peel away the waxed paper, handling the sugar lace gently. Use these pieces on the top edge of an iced cake; secure them to the cake with a dab of royal icing. To arrange these pieces in a standing position, prop them with tissue paper until set; avoid moving the work for several hours.

When doing lace work it is a good idea to make some spares in case breakages occur.

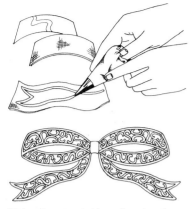

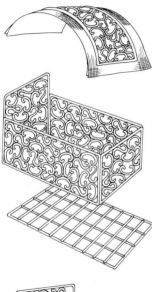

Piping the separate pieces for a lace bow.

Shaped net pieces

To make a bow Cut a piece of tin, about 2 inches (5 cm.) wide and 6 inches (15 cm.) long, with snips or strong kitchen scissors into the shape required and bend it to an arc shape. Cover with waxed paper and then cotton net. Pipe lines about $1\frac{1}{2}$ inches ($3\frac{1}{2}$ cm.) apart and 5 inches (13 cm.) long on the curved surface. Fill the centre of this rectangle with a lacy pattern and leave to dry. Make three more pieces in the same way for the two loops of the bows.

Cut and bend a piece of tin in the form of a wave shape. Cover with waxed paper and net and pipe a lace work strip in the same way as for the loops. Make one end V shaped and the other end pointed to represent the end of the ribbon. Make a second piece in the same way. When all six pieces are dry, arrange them on a finished cake in the shape of a bow.

To make a net and icing lace cot

Make the curved base on the side of a cocoa tin. Make the bottom, two sides, head and foot on net on waxed paper. Leave aside to dry.

Fasten the two sides to the ends by piping a line of royal icing inside. Pipe a row of royal icing around the bottom and place the cot sides in position. Leave until set. Arrange the curved base on the cake with a little icing to hold it in place at the ends and carefully place the cot piece on top. Use net on all these pieces and trim off any surplus carefully with a pair of sharp scissors.

To make a baby for the cot

Add a little more sugar to $\frac{1}{2}$ teaspoon royal icing until it is stiff enough to form a ball about the size of a pea. When quite dry, use an artist's fine brush and brown food colouring to paint fine lines to represent hair on the ball of icing. Similarly paint two dots for eyes in blue and a tiny rosebud mouth in red. This should be very simply done, do not try to make an elaborate painting of a face.

To make a cot coverlet

Pipe an oblong on waxed paper about $\frac{1}{4}$ inch ($\frac{1}{2}$ cm.) by 1 inch ($2\frac{1}{2}$ cm.) and fill this oblong with rather thin royal icing; allow to dry overnight. This can be used as a pillow in the cot. Place the ball to represent the baby's head on a dab of icing on the pillow. For the coverlet, pipe a piece of icing on waxed paper 1 inch ($2\frac{1}{2}$ cm.) wide and $1\frac{3}{4}$ inches (4 cm.) long in the same way as for the pillow. When quite dry, lift from the waxed paper and place in the cot carefully so that the top comes up against the ball that represents the head. A body is not necessary. If wished, the coverlet may be decorated with white or pale coloured lace work and a tiny looped edge before placing it in the cot. If necessary add a

The separate pieces ready to be assembled for a net and icing lace cot.

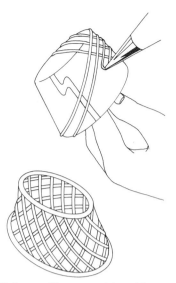

Piping a trellis on a special mould to make a basket.

A garden trug basket made by first piping the separate lace pieces on the side of a cocoa tin.

A completed basket. The handle is made over a suitably shaped mould by piping a trellis. The basket is filled with moulded roses.

touch of icing at the top of the cot cover to neaten any space.

It is always worthwhile making all these pieces in duplicate from the beginning in case of breakages, as it is almost as quick to make two at once than to re-make a broken piece. Great care is necessary in handling these pieces, and all lace work.

To make a basket

Make a fine trellis or lace work basket to hold flowers, by following the method for trellis work, on a suitably shaped mould. (It is possible to buy moulds in pink plastic.) To work a trellis on a mould with the top outer rim wider than the bottom outer rim, it is advisable to work sloping lines each side, and then to fill in the quarter lines to ensure that the remaining spaces are even. The lines at the top will naturally be a little wider apart than those at the bottom.

The lace pattern is far easier to work on this type of mould, but remember to strengthen the edge with tiny stars or whipping, and then leave to dry.

A garden trug basket can be made on the side of a cocoa tin, using the length and half the width around for the main part of the basket, and half the round top and bottom of the tin for the ends of the basket. Leave the three separate pieces to dry, and then fix together. Many different shaped ornaments can be made and fastened together in this way.

To make a handle for the basket Grease a similar shaped mould, the correct size for a handle to fit the basket. Work two lines over the greased mould, and join with criss-cross trellis or lace work using the usual letters – 'x', 'c and 's'. When quite dry, remove the mould if possible using the hot water method, or, hold the icing handle near to a source of heat and support it in the hand until the grease melts and the icing can be carefully taken from the mould. It is advisable to make several spare handles when doing this fine work, as breakages are frequent.

To assemble the basket, fill the bottom with a little cotton wool and fill up with tiny sugar flowers or almond paste fruits. Put a star of icing on each side of the top of the basket and carefully place the handle in position. Support with crushed tissue paper until the join is dry and firm.

These baskets can be used as a centrepiece for a birthday cake, and the lace work varied by colouring the icing. Using the same method, make a small trellis or lace work cradle. Work half the mould to make the cradle hood. Fix to one end of the complete basket shape, to resemble the cradle.

To make a lace triangle cake

Cut out a circle of greaseproof paper the same size as the cake top, using the cake tin as a guide, or measuring the cake across and using a pair of compasses to make the circle. Divide the circle into

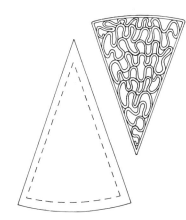

Zig-zag lace work. These sections are first piped on to pieces of waxed paper fastened on to glass.

Lace triangles used to decorate a cake covered with coloured sugar paste.

the number of pieces of lace work needed – eight is an easy number to work with.

Cut out the sections of paper carefully, and put on to a piece of glass, fastening the corners with a very little icing from a tube. Cover the sections with triangular pieces of thin waxed paper a little bigger than the greaseproof triangles which should show through the waxed paper. Again, fasten down at the corners with a little icing and outline each piece of greaseproof showing through the wax paper with a No. 1 tube. Fill the centres of each of these triangles with the letters 'x', 'c' and 's' or with zig-zag lace work. Also make small triangles for the edges of the cake having the base of each either equal to the top triangles, or half their size. Here again, make a few extra in case of breakages. Leave all the triangles until completely dry.

To remove the lace, place over the edge of a book or a box edge, and carefully bring the waxed paper downwards peeling it away from the icing.

A cake suitable for this type of decoration should have a plain, flat surface in white or coloured royal icing or sugar paste. As there is so much work involved in decorating this cake, use a rich fruit cake that will keep well. Tie a ribbon or silver braid around the cake, or use decorative piping. Roll a ball of sugar paste into a 1-inch (2½-cm.) marble shape, or if royal icing is used, add enough sugar to make a very stiff mixture, and roll into a ball, leaving on waxed paper to dry.

When dry, place the ball, or any other suitable ornament in the centre of the cake, and place the large triangles carefully balancing them between the cake edge and the ball, pointing into the centre. Pipe a row of royal icing stars around the edge of the cake, seven or eight at a time. Place the small triangle in the soft stars, pointing downwards and outwards, one or two to every large top triangle. Similarly, pipe a row of stars around the bottom edge of the cake, again only piping seven or eight at a time. Put in small triangles opposite each of the top edge triangles, raised a little, not resting flat on the board. For the design using two small triangles to one large one, put in a row of triangles around the bottom edge opposite those around the top edge, and a second row nearer the board, but still raised slightly from the board.

Although it is always wise to follow the advice given earlier, and make a few extra triangles, it is amazing how few breakages actually occur once experience has been gained.

To make a lace trellis collar cake

To make the collar A pair of compasses and a sheet of perfectly smooth greaseproof paper will be needed if this circular sugar lace trellis is to be worked accurately. There must be absolutely no creases or fold marks in the greaseproof paper.

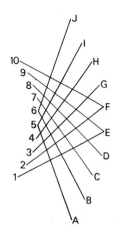

A diagram showing how to work a lace trellis collar. The collar is worked by piping a line from point 1 to point E, from point 5 to point A and continuing to pipe lines next to each other, following alternately the first line made and then the second one until the circle is completed.

A cake decorated with a lace trellis collar and a nativity scene in the centre.

Draw a circle on the paper, the diameter of which is 1 inch (2½ cm.) larger than the diameter of the cake and a second circle inside the first, 1 inch (2½ cm.) less than the diameter of the cake. This will give a collar 1 inch (2½ cm.) wide all round, which will jut ½ inch (1 cm.) over the outer edge of the cake, and will be supported by the ½ inch (1 cm.) overlapping the cake. If compasses are not available, two suitable sized plates can be used.

Mark dots ¼ inch (½ cm.) apart round the inside of the greaseproof paper ring. Directly opposite one of these dots, mark a corresponding dot just inside the outer circle. Repeat on the opposite side of the outer circle, and at quarter positions, and then fill in dots evenly spaced on the outside circle until there is one corresponding to each one on the inner circle although naturally those on the outer circle will be spaced farther apart. Fasten the paper ring on to a piece of glass with a little icing, and cover with a smooth sheet of thin waxed paper. The waxed paper should also be fastened with dabs of icing.

Using a No. 1 tube and well beaten royal icing, pipe a line from a dot on the inner circle to a dot on the outer circle (point 1 to point E in the line drawing). Ice a second line, beginning on the inner circle at point 5, directly opposite point E, and joining point 5 to point A on the outer circle. This makes a start, the lines crossing in the middle. Continue making lines next to each other, following alternately the first line made, and then the second line made, until the circle is completed. The finish of the work will join up neatly, but it will always be visible.

When the trellis lines are completed, add a row of dots close together around the inner circle for neatening and strengthening. Leave the work in a warm place for several days until quite dry. Remove the waxed paper very gently and carefully by peeling from the back of the lace work with the majority of the ring resting on the edge of a table. Peel off a little at a time so that the waxed paper is removed only very slowly.

To finish the cake Complete the decoration on the cake before adding the lace collar, by making dainty poinsettias (see page 41) in almond or sugar paste coloured red. Make leaves from green almond or sugar paste and mark with a knife or skewer. Add a few pieces of asparagus fern and pipe yellow icing in the centre of the poinsettias for a realistic effect. Place a small flower and some fern on the sides of the cake, and small red florets at intervals on the board round the base. Circle the top edge of the cake with a narrow red ribbon.

To complete the board Mark out the base of the cake and the cake board with dots in the same way as the greaseproof ring was marked for the top collar. Ice a trellis following the same directions. The dots on the cake should be about ½ inch (1 cm.) up the side of the cake. Touch the cake first with the tube, and bring the line of icing out long enough to reach the dots on the board, and then finish off. The hanging curve of icing must be the same length each time. Neaten the lines of trellis with dots of icing.

Final stage When the decoration on the cake has reached this point, lift the trellis collar very carefully from the paper on to the cake. Secure here and there on the inner edge with tiny dots of icing. Finally, add tiny hanging loops on the collar edge.

To make a lace trellis top for a cake

Before attempting to begin a trellis top, the design must be worked out on greaseproof paper to ensure absolute accuracy. Using a pair of compasses, divide the circumference of a circle of grease-proof paper the same size as the cake, into five equal sections, marking each with a dot. Freehand, draw in the design. Cut the pattern into five pieces, which should all be the same and shaped as the line drawing.

Place these five greaseproof paper patterns on a piece of glass, cover with slightly larger pieces of waxed paper, and fasten down at the corners with a dab of icing. Make sure that these dots of icing will not come under the trellis work.

Outline the shape of the five pieces with a No. 1 tube, and begin working from the top right-hand point to the outer edge directly opposite the top left-hand point. Continue working lines parallel to each other, and $\frac{1}{8}$ inch ($\frac{1}{4}$ cm.) apart, working across the pattern from right to left. When this is completed, work the trellis by making lines in the opposite way, from left to right. Complete the five pieces, strengthening the inside edges with dots placed close together. Make one or two extra patterns in case of breakage. Leave these pieces to dry well in a warm place.

The top of the cake should have a good flat smooth surface of icing. The sides should have a narrow band of deep blue ribbon around the centre, and two narrow bands of silver paper braid cut to the right width and placed each side of the ribbon. Make about five deep blue forget-me-nots using a petal tube and icing to match the deep blue ribbon. Place these on the centre of the cake with dainty sprigs of asparagus fern. Fasten in position with a little icing from the tube.

Remove the pale blue trellis from the waxed paper by peeling it away over the edge of a book. Place it in position on the cake over small stars or dots of icing placed at the corner positions to raise the trellis a little from the cake.

Using white royal icing and a large star tube, make long scrolls, starting thick in the middle of each of the five patterns, and gradually thinning out at the points where one piece joins the next. Neaten the join with a large star and with three graduated stars underneath it, extending over the silver band round the side of the cake. Repeat these same long scrolls on the board at the base of the cake and continue the stars at each join with three graduated stars out on to the board.

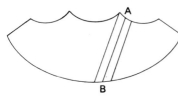

When working the lace trellis for the top of the cake shown in the picture on this page, begin by piping the lines from A to B.

A cake showing the top decorated with a very fine lace trellis.

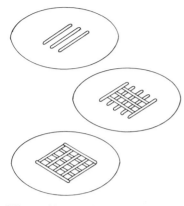

When making a cushion to be used on the edge of a square or round cake, begin by piping three short lines in the centre; cross these with three more lines at an angle of 45°. Continue in this way until the cushion is a suitable size for the cake.

A cake decorated with three cushions, and crossing hanging loops.

To make a cushion

Cushions are a different form of raised work, used on the edges of either square or round cakes. The lines are built up on each other, beginning with three small lines in the centre, then three more crossing the first at an angle of 45°. Continue in this way, working over the first three lines and making an extra line at each side, and then working over the second three lines, adding an extra line each side. Work first one way and then the other, each time over-piping the original lines and adding two new lines, aiming at an oval shape. If necessary, put a guide line over the edge of the cake before starting. The trellis lines are worked exactly over each other as the building up progresses, so that the cake can always be seen through the lines. This is very effective worked with coloured icing, as the number of lines worked over each other appear to deepen the colour at the centre.

This work needs much practice and should always be carried out on the edge of a practice board before working on the actual cake. It is not so easily broken as work done over a greased mould, and it is very suitable placed over the edge of a cake where a dome shape cannot be used. As the work proceeds, it may be necessary to tidy up the edges with a knife, as a good shape is most important. Neaten the finished cushion with a row of tiny stars or with a piped line.

To make a crinoline lady lace cake

This is a cake for a special occasion as it entails quite a lot of work. The sugar lace pattern can be your own design or made up from the drawing given. The sugar lace pattern is worked on a round basin the same size as the cake is baked in.

Bake a rich fruit cake mixture in a basin. Cover the cooled cake with almond paste and royal icing – one coat is sufficient – and place on a silver board to dry. Grease the outside of the basin and work the lace pattern in a circle around the bottom of the basin and allow to dry overnight in a warm room. Warm the basin by pouring in hot water, then carefully remove the lace frill. Place over the cake and to the bottom of the cake on the silver board. Neaten the top edge of the frill with icing. Wash the basin and re-grease the outer surface. Repeat with a second lace icing frill on the basin higher up but so that the frill will fit in place on the cake lady. This time make a row of dots of icing to hold the frill in place when it is slipped over the cake. Continue in this way until the cake is covered with frills. Arrange the china head in place (or model a head and body from modelling fondant). Decorate with narrow ribbon and a rose and fan made separately on waxed paper.

The frills for this cake take several days to make; it is advanced work and great care is needed, but it is a challenge for keen cake decorators.

The detail of a sugar lace pattern which can be used for a crinoline lady lace cake or a lace petal dress lady.

To make a lace petal dress lady

Bake a cake mixture as for the crinoline lady lace cake. Measure around the base of the cake and make as many lace motifs as the number of inches around the cake for the base, this for the bottom row of points. Measure the depth of the cake and calculate how many motifs will be required at 1 inch (2½ cm.) above each other, remembering each row will take a few less motifs. Make a number of patterns from the drawing given and cover with wax paper. Pipe over the drawings, using a No. 1 tube and white or coloured royal icing, on the waxed paper. Allow these to dry thoroughly. Remove from the paper and store in a box on cotton wool.

Using a small star tube in a paper icing bag, make a row of icing around the base of the cake 1 inch (2½ cm.) up from the cake board. Place the lace motifs, close together all round the base of the cake, into this row of icing whilst it is wet. Make another row of icing with the star tube barely 1 inch (2½ cm.) higher over the first row of lace petals and arrange a second row of lace motifs. Continue in this way until the whole cake is covered. Finally place the china head in position with icing underneath.

Lace butterflies

Trace the drawing of a butterfly shown on page 188, or use your own design. Make two wings and so that the wings are in pairs turn the drawing over when tracing a second wing to make a right and left one. Cover the drawing with waxed paper and pipe in white or coloured royal icing using a No. 1 or 2 tube. The wings can be made stronger by filling in some parts of the wings to be solid with run-out thin royal icing (see page 132).

To use lace butterflies Pipe the shape of the body on waxed paper or straight on to the cake using royal icing and a bag with a hole cut to the same size as a No. 3 tube. Place the lace wings in a standing position in the wet icing body. Prop these with crushed tissue paper until dry. Pipe in the antennae with a No. 1 tube flat on the cake, or on waxed paper; when dry, arrange on a dot of icing in a raised position on the head of the butterfly.

A lace butterfly strengthened with run-out icing; run-out teddy bear and pansies.

Lace work numbers and letters

In the same way draw or trace a design from a book containing patterns of letters or numbers, or draw one freehand and fasten down on the board. Cover with waxed paper and pipe the outline of the figure or letter in royal icing using a No. 1 tube. Pipe trellis lines parallel to each other in the outlining. Over-pipe the outlining to give a neat finish and complete with tiny dots all around the edge. When dry lift these letters carefully and arrange on the cake on a neat bed of icing in a standing position. Prop up until dry with crushed tissue paper, or if the letters are to be flat, a dot of icing at the edges of the letters of figures is sufficient just to raise them a fraction above the cake.

Pastillage work and modelling

A book on cake decorating would not be complete without mentioning pastillage. This is a French word which comes from pastille which is a firm jelly-type gum sweet. Pastillage can be used for piping, modelling or like pastry for making strong pieces of icing for building models.

Pastillage 1

½ teaspoon gum tragacanth
4 heaped tablespoons royal icing

Stir the gum into the icing and leave it to stand for about 1 hour, covered with a damp cloth. Pipe with this icing as if using royal icing. It is excellent for piping ornaments for the top of a wedding cake, sugar baskets, or any decoration which requires to be strong as the icing dries very hard.

Pastillage for modelling figures

For modelling figures make up the pastillage, as above; cover with a wet cloth and then put the container with the pastillage and wet cover in a polythene bag to prevent drying out. Leave to stand overnight. The next day mix well and add enough sifted icing sugar to make the mixture very stiff; knead well until smooth.

Use for making white roses for decorating wedding cakes using the method for almond paste roses described on page 39. Use cornflour for rolling out the pastillage and as a dusting for the fingers. Work fast as the paste sets hard quickly and will crack and leave a poor surface unless care is taken. Store these roses in an airtight container on cotton wool (or in an egg box) until required for use.

This paste can also be used for modelling small animals and figures, wedding bells, cupids etc. which should be white in colour for wedding cakes. If the surface is cracked the paste has too much sugar in or too much time has been taken during the making, allowing the paste to dry out. Add a little more royal icing and work well kneading it in by hand; cover the pastillage with a damp cloth.

Pastillage 2

IMPERIAL/METRIC

1 teaspoon gelatine
1½ tablespoons cold water
1 tablespoon granulated sugar
1 tablespoon liquid glucose
about 1 lb./450 g. icing sugar,
   sifted

Soak the gelatine in the water in a basin for about 20 minutes. Stir and add the granulated sugar. Place the basin in a pan of hot (not boiling) water and stir until the sugar has dissolved. Stir in the glucose. Add icing sugar until paste is required consistency.

Use the paste for piping out ornaments; make it a little stiffer (by adding more icing sugar) for moulding into flowers and figures; make it stiffer still for rolling out to make sheets of paste for making cards, wheelbarrows, model houses or other buildings. Roll out on cornflour. Dry on a flat surface – a sheet of glass dusted with cornflour.

Pastillage 3

IMPERIAL/METRIC

2 teaspoons gelatine
2 teaspoons cold water
2 teaspoons hot water
1 teaspoon white cooking fat
2 teaspoons gum tragacanth
about 1 lb./450 g. icing sugar,
    sifted

Soak the gelatine in the cold water in a basin for about 10 minutes. Add the hot water, then place the basin in a pan of hot (not boiling) water until the gelatine has completely dissolved. Remove from the heat and add the white fat and gum tragacanth. Gradually beat in some of the icing sugar – enough to make a stiff, firm mixture. Knead the mixture by hand, then roll it into a ball and place in a greased polythene bag. Place the polythene bag in an airtight container and leave to stand overnight before using. If storing the pastillage for any length of time, keep it in the refrigerator. Bring it to room temperature before using again for all kinds of moulded work.

Moulding paste for sugar animals

IMPERIAL/METRIC

1 teaspoon gelatine
1½ teaspoons water
1 teaspoon white cooking fat
1½–2 lb./675–900 g. icing sugar,
    sifted
food colouring (optional)

Soak the gelatine in the water in a small pan for 1 hour; add the fat and, stirring, heat slowly to simmering point. Pour on to 1½ lb. (675 g.) sifted icing sugar. Mix well and knead in more sifted icing sugar to make the required stiffness for moulding into sugar animals. Dust the hands with cornflour before moulding the animals.

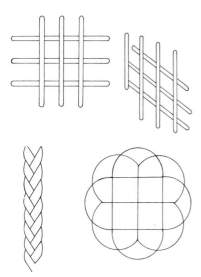

To make a tragacanth basket, first pipe lines with icing strengthened with tragacanth (pastillage 1) across the base of the mould. Cross these lines either diagonally or at right angles. Now make loops as shown. A handle may be made by piping a plait or a straight line and the completed basket may be filled with sweets, chocolates or piped or moulded flowers.

Tragacanth baskets *Also illustrated on pages 30 and 59*
Grease the outside of a small mould – e.g. a ramekin dish – generously with lard or cooking fat. Make particularly sure that the edges are well greased. Using a large paper icing bag, pastillage 1 (see opposite) and a No. 5 star tube, pipe lines about ½ inch (1 cm.) apart across the base to the edge of the mould. Cross these lines either diagonally or at right angles.

Turn the mould upside down, and with the base at the top, make hanging loops around the outside of the mould, leaving 1 inch (2½ cm.) between the ends. The second loop should overlap the first, as in the line drawing. Continue making overlapping loops in this way, so that the distance between the ends is now ½ inch (1 cm.), until the last loop is completed. Make a ring of icing around the base of the mould with the star tube, neatening the loop ends. Leave for several days to dry in a warm, heated room.

If necessary, make a handle for the basket by piping a line over the centre of the outside of a similar shaped greased mould. Either work a straight line, or a plait. Avoid making a plait too thick, although the edges must touch each other.

When both the basket and the handle are quite dry, remove from the mould. Hold the icing in the hollow of the left hand, supported by the fingers. Carefully pour hot water from the kettle into the mould. This melts the fat, and a tinkling noise will

121

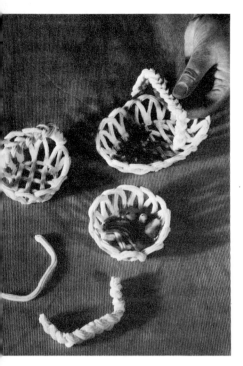

Tragacanth baskets.

A cake decorated with a pastillage card showing a painting of Greenwich Church.

be heard. Lift the mould from the sugar basket. Take care over this, particularly when removing the handle. In both cases, avoid allowing the water to run down the sides of the mould, as it would immediately melt the icing and cause it to break.

To complete the basket Fill with almond paste fruits, sweets or chocolates, or arrange with ferns and almond paste flowers. Make two stars opposite each other on the edge of the basket, and place the handle in position. Support with tissue paper until quite firm and dry. Do not attempt to lift the basket by the handle. Store in a dry place until required.

Sugar dishes as a dinner party sweet

Make baskets as described on page 121, some in white icing, and some coloured and flavoured with vanilla essence or peppermint, etc. Do not make any handles. Have some firm ice cream in the refrigerator and the sugar baskets ready on plates. To serve, quickly cut the block of ice cream into pieces and place a piece in each sugar dish. Top with a cherry or a sugar flower. This makes a specially unusual dinner party sweet.

When using the baskets in this way, do not attempt to make handles. If preferred, these baskets can be made without adding the tragacanth to the royal icing but the baskets will not be so hard and very great care will be needed in handling them.

Edible Christmas cards and plaques in pastillage
Also illustrated on page 95

An edible Christmas card is a unique gift and fascinating to make. The royal icing should be well beaten, and again, add $\frac{1}{2}$ teaspoon tragacanth to 4 tablespoons icing. Leave to stand overnight. Mix well and add as much sifted icing sugar as can be absorbed. Knead well, using a little cornflour on the hands to prevent the mixture sticking. Lightly dredge the board and rolling pin with cornflour, and begin to roll out a piece of the mixture, now known as gum paste or pastillage. Roll out evenly to about $\frac{1}{8}$ inch ($\frac{1}{4}$ cm.) in thickness and, using a ruler as a guide, cut into two equal oblongs. Place on a sheet of glass evenly dredged with cornflour to prevent sticking.

With a large plain tube (about No. 4), cut two holes in the sides of each sheet of pastillage, ready to take the Christmas card ribbon. Work quickly, or the pastillage will set and crack.

Any pieces not used should be kept under a cloth while working on another section. The remaining pieces can be kneaded again, rolled out and cut into round plaques with a biscuit cutter. Never waste any pastillage. Every little piece can be utilised. Small pieces make useful plaques for birthday cakes or for hanging on a Christmas tree. Paint a design on them with food colouring, or flavour them with peppermint essence and cut into tiny sweets. Write on the larger ones, and use them as a Hallowe'en novelty.

To make the picture on a pastillage card

If one is quite artistic there will be no difficulty in using food colouring to paint a picture or design, freehand, on to a sugar Christmas or Easter card or plaque. For those who are not quite so artistic, a simple tracing method can be used.

Find a card or picture in a book, the right size for use on the piece of pastillage. Make a tracing on greaseproof paper and then outline the tracing on the back of the greaseproof, using graphite or black lead pencil. These are not harmful if eaten but never use a ballpoint pen or copying ink. Place the tracing on the sugar card or plaque, pressing only lightly on the sheet of pastillage or gum paste to prevent it breaking. It is important to make sure that the sugar card is completely dry and flat. Outline the tracing again, remove the paper, and a fine outline should remain on the pastillage. Colour in the picture with an artist's fine brush and a little food colouring, mixing the colours to the chosen shade. There is rarely any need to buy more than the three primary colours, yellow, blue and red, as a mixture of these will produce any other colour that may be needed – blue and yellow making green, blue and red making purple, yellow and red making orange, and all three mixed to varying degrees forming black and browns. To make the colours a lighter shade, simply add more water. It is advisable to try out a colour first on a small piece of pastillage before beginning a large, important piece of work.

Never worry about making an exact copy of the original picture. This is not always possible on sugar, and perhaps this is a good thing. A very good effect can be achieved, and when after some time, the original has been forgotten and the sugar picture is studied again, the result is often more pleasing than an exact copy. Quite often a latent talent is discovered in this way.

For the best results, use a fairly dry brush for painting on the food colouring. A wet brush is liable to melt the sugar surface which then becomes sticky. This technique becomes a lot easier with more practice.

To complete the Christmas card Write some simple greetings on the second piece of prepared pastillage, place the picture piece on top, and thread a piece of fine ribbon through the holes. Tie in a neat but loose bow, otherwise the card cannot be opened. Arrange in a suitable sized box lined with a thin piece of cotton wool, or use as a centrepiece on a cake.

A pastillage book

A small open book can quite easily be made by rolling out the pastillage to the size needed, and drying the two sides over a slightly rounded surface of a rolling pin or a jar dusted with cornflour. Rub the pastillage gently with a little cornflour on the finger, leave for one to two days to dry, then brush away any surplus cornflour before beginning to colour in a picture. Arrange

A Christmas cake decorated with a pastillage book, and holly made from almond paste.

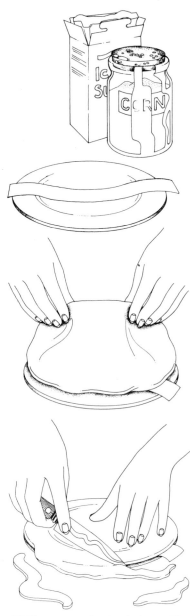

the two pieces together to form a book.

Take special care tracing a picture on to the curved surface, or the pastillage will break. Press only very lightly, or support the book from underneath. Using an artist's fine brush, only lightly dampened with food colouring, write suitable wording on one side of the pastillage page and paint a small design or picture on the other. If the book is to be used on a cake, place in position and fix with a little royal icing underneath.

Sugar plates and dishes *Illustrated on pages 30 and 103*

Make these by combining the methods of making a plaque and those of making a sugar basket. Complete a pastillage plaque as explained previously, and when it is dry, paint a picture on it with food colouring. Place on a china plate, fancy dish or mould, dusted with cornflour and a strip of waxed paper placed underneath so that it is easier to lift later. Grease the uncovered outer edges of the plate or dish and pipe a lace work design from the plaque, making sure the icing joins on to the edge of the plaque. Add a pinch of tragacanth to the icing used for the piping.

Remove the sugar plate by warming it gently over a source of heat, and carefully slipping off the mould. Arrange two or three almond paste fruits, or chocolates on the plate, and use as a table decoration or a party novelty.

Sugar boxes *Illustrated on page 103*

For the most attractive effect, make these from coloured pastillage, by kneading in some colouring thoroughly, or using coloured icing to make the pastillage. Blue is perhaps the most attractive colour, as boxes of blue pastillage can be made to resemble Wedgwood china.

Cut paper patterns for complete accuracy. Make four for the sides of the box, one to fit in as a base, and one for the lid. If necessary, make patterns for lid edges at the same time. Sprinkle the board with cornflour, roll out the coloured pastillage to $\frac{1}{8}$ inch ($\frac{1}{4}$ cm.) thick, and place the paper pattern on the paste, working quickly so that the pastillage does not set before the pattern is removed. Cut round the patterns with a sharp pointed knife, place the pieces on glass dredged with cornflour and leave to set.

Using a No. 1 tube and white or coloured royal icing, decorate the pieces of pastillage with designs of trellis, hanging loops or polka dots. Again, leave to dry thoroughly, and then put the box together. Begin by fixing the two opposite ends of the box to the base, using royal icing from the tube. Stand on cornflour and prop up with tissue paper or a jam jar until quite dry. When dry, fix the second two sides in position in the same way. The lid should be left until last, it can be separate, or fixed with icing to the box at an attractive half-open angle. Small run-out Wedgwood figures (see page 125) can be made to decorate the box.

Making a sugar plate by placing pastillage on a plate dusted with cornflour. To ensure that the sugar plate will come off the mould, arrange a strip of waxed paper across the mould. This plate could be made with pastillage coloured blue and decorated with Wedgwood-type figures.

Wedgwood-design wedding cakes *Illustrated on pages 99 and 102*
This design is very popular and makes an attractive wedding cake.

The first coat of royal icing for the cake should be white so that it can be sandpapered to obtain a perfectly smooth surface. The second and third coat must be in a Wedgwood blue colour and as these will not be able to be sandpapered as the sugar grains would be broken and make scratches, they must be applied with great care. Therefore this is a design for someone who has mastered the art of making a good flat surface.

To make freehand figures for Wedgwood work

Make a tracing of the outline of the figure from a Wedgwood vase or catalogue picture. Cover the tracing with waxed paper and pipe the outline with royal icing. Fill in the centre with soft piping icing, up and down, for the folds of the dress etc. Press smooth parts of the figure with the finger or a slightly dampened artist's fine brush.

All kinds of figures can be copied in this way. Wedgwood figures can also be made in a mould (see page 173). Standing figures should be piped back and front.

All Wedgwood-type figures should be made in royal icing, well in advance and stored on cotton wool together with any other royal icing decorations made.

Raised surfaces on plaques and cards

Sometimes a second small plaque can be placed on top of a larger plaque to give a raised surface. The second plaque should be made as thinly as possible, so that the sugar is not too hard to eat – if any of these sugar novelties are a little hard, steam from a boiling kettle, or a short time in a damp atmosphere will soon soften the icing. It is often advisable to paint the second plaque when it has been set in position, as the very lightest pressure could crack the thin pastillage if there is nothing to support it.

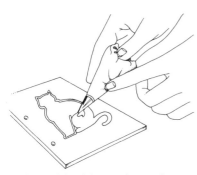

Soft royal icing being run-in to make a figure outlined on a sheet of pastillage.

A figure can be outlined on pastillage and then filled with soft royal icing as when making ladies' fingers (see page 97). When set, paint in details, with food colouring, of hair and features.

To make a birthday cake using pastillage

To prepare the cake For this design, the edge of the cake must be well angled with very little or no bevel on the top edge. Measure the circumference of the cake, and work out the size needed for each trellis work circle – these should be made four large and four small, leaving a 1-inch ($2\frac{1}{2}$-cm.) space between each one.

Draw the eight circles on thin cardboard with a pair of compasses. Cut through the centre and place in position on the cake. Use as templates for icing both the top and the sides of the cake, and secure the pieces of cardboard to the sides with pins, or a dot of icing.

Pipe a line around the cardboard circles and remove them from the cake. Next, using a No. 1 tube, pipe the trellis, working lines parallel to the edge of the cake and when these are completed, cross them at right angles over the side of the cake, beginning with a line from the middle of one top semi-circle to the middle of the semi-circle below. To do this successfully, it may be helpful to tilt the cake. Neaten the edges of the circles, and the edges of the cake in between the circles, with a small star tube.

The next step is to ice dots marking the position of the hanging loops. When the loops are complete, finish with five dots in each loop, and three dots between each loop. Lastly, work trellis lines over a layer of set white icing which has been put on the board, from the base of the cake to the board edge, working the lines all one way first, and then crossing with lines all going the other way. Remember that the outer edge of the board will be slightly wider than the inner edge, and a little bit of graduating will be needed. Neaten between the board and the cake with a row of small stars.

To make the birthday card Roll out the pastillage following the directions on page 122. Cut two pieces of a suitable size and make small holes for the ribbon. Dry on glass sprinkled with cornflour. When the pastillage is completely set, pipe a small vase, using a No. 1 icing tube. With practice, this can be done freehand. Fill in the vase with trellis lines and neaten by outlining again. Using a ribbon tube, pipe a garland of pale blue icing for

A birthday cake decorated with a pastillage card.

126

the ribbon. When the garland is dry, write Birthday Greetings in deeper blue icing, using a No. 0 or 00 tube. Make some tiny pink roses in two shades on a cocktail stick or a pin head, allow to dry on waxed paper, and then place in position on the card face. Write a greeting inside the card, using pale blue icing and a No. 0 tube, and tie the two pages of the card together loosely with blue ribbon to match the icing. Put a dab of icing on the back of the card and place in position.

Place a single rose between the slightly opened card to prevent the top page crushing the piped writing inside.

A Christmas cake with pastillage plaque

To make the picture, take a tracing from a Christmas card, and trace it out on to a plaque of pastillage, colouring as explained on page 123.

A Christmas cake decorated with a pastillage plaque.

Fold a circle of paper the same size as the cake surface into eight equal parts; mark it out to an eight-point star, and then round off the inner edges. From this paper pattern, make a template of cardboard. Place the template in the centre of the cake and work around it.

To make the trellis, begin by piping a line from the centre of each hollow, to the edge of the cake, and filling in with parallel lines. Cross these at right angles with lines beginning with a single line from one star point to the next. Complete the shape with two more curved lines outlining the pattern, building up the middle line once more, and the outer line three times. Place the plaque in position, a little to the top, leaving room to write greetings below. Arrange a ring of almond paste holly around the plaque.

Finish by making hanging loops from point to point around the side of the cake, decorating with a lily pattern, and making a shell edge around the base of the cake and round the top edge, using a No. 5 star tube, or larger if preferred.

A cake with a central dome

This is an interestingly-designed cake, with the pastillage work half hidden in the centre under a lace work dome (see page 109). The plaque can be designed for almost any event, showing a school badge, a message, greetings, or a picture of some particular season or event.

Cut a thin cardboard template in the same way as for the Christmas cake and work the outer line of the design. Remove the template and repeat the pattern line three times, making the middle line two rows deep, and the outer line three deep. Inside the inner pattern line, follow the design with a line of dots, adding eight short rows of dots from each point to the centre piece.

A cake decorated with a central dome and four cushions.

In the centre of each top edge, work a cushion, neatening each one with a shell edge. Put double hanging loops from each of the cushions, and add hanging dots between the loops. Tie a coloured ribbon around the centre of the cake. Make 12 roses on cocktail sticks to match the colour of the ribbon, and add several pull-out leaves. When dry, arrange these in position at the corners. Arrange the plaque in position, with the lace dome placed over it. Hold the dome in position with an edging of shells.

Whiten the board with icing and, when dry, cover neatly with braiding and finish with a long scroll at the base of the cake. Two or three shells neaten the corners of a square cake.

Freehand piping on plaques *Illustrated on page 98*
Some of the most attractive scenes involve animals. These can be drawn freehand or traced on to a pastillage plaque which has been allowed to dry thoroughly. Once the basic outline has been transferred to the pastillage the detail can be worked in – this type of work is known as raised royal icing or *shaggy work*.

Using a bag only, cut to the size of a No. 1 tube, and royal icing, make lines (as if using a paint brush) to represent the animal's hair. Work in white or coloured icing, choosing the palest colour on the animal, as the darkest colours can be painted in with a brush. Work over the first row of icing to build up the body of the animal and give it shape. In this way, quite elaborate pictures can be built up using a number of bags of coloured icing at the same time. Obviously this comes more easily to anyone with an artistic tendency, but it is amazing what can be achieved by almost anyone, once the attempt has been made.

Pastillage flowers
Pastillage is particularly good for making flowers, as it can be pressed out very thinly and sets quickly, so that the petals hold their shape well. Pastillage takes any colour well whereas with flowers made from almond paste it is not possible to colour the paste a delicate pink. Pastillage is especially indispensable for making pure white or very pale pink roses for wedding cakes.

To make white roses
Pastillage for roses is made up in exactly the same way as it is for making cards or plaques. Make a cone about $\frac{3}{4}$ inch ($1\frac{1}{2}$ cm.) high and $\frac{1}{2}$ inch (1 cm.) wide at the base. Roll out a small piece of pastillage to an $\frac{1}{8}$ inch ($\frac{1}{4}$ cm.) in thickness. (Keep the paste not in use covered with a cloth.) Cut only one small round at a time for each petal, using a sharp round cutter. If several are cut at a time, the edges of the petals will tend to crack. Thin out the circle of pastillage between the thumb and finger until it is paper thin. Using a little water on a fine brush, dampen the base of the petal, then fold it around the cone, completely enclosing it. Cut a second circle and, leaving the base thick, thin out the top of the petal with the thumb and finger. Dampen the thick base slightly with a brush and place at the back of the first petal.

Continue adding as many petals as necessary, curling over the final petals slightly. Prop with tissue paper to keep the shape. It is possible to produce a good effect with as few as four, five or six petals, in fact more should not really be needed. Work quickly as this paste soon becomes too hard to model.

It is always advisable, before trying to make good model roses, to look at some real roses in the garden, or realistic pictures.

To make coloured roses

Knead a little colour into the pastillage, then follow the directions for making white roses. Two-coloured roses can also be made by using a piece of white or pale yellow and a piece of pink pastillage, both rolled out until about $\frac{1}{4}$ inch ($\frac{1}{2}$ cm.) thick, and then placed on top of one another and rolled together until the paste is $\frac{1}{8}$ inch ($\frac{1}{4}$ cm.) thick, pink on one side, and white or yellow on the other. Cut out circles as if making white roses and put together as before. Aim at making the finished flower suitably shaped for adding a few leaves at the back. Prop the roses with tissue paper until quite dry.

To make Christmas roses

Roll out the pastillage and cut out very small circles. Press out evenly all over, and prop up the petals on tissue paper, curving them slightly. When dry, tint each petal very lightly with streaks of pale pink or green at the base. Make a knob of icing on waxed paper and insert five or six dry petals to form a flower. Have ready some stamens, made by piping lengths of pale yellow or white with a No. 1 tube on to waxed paper. Tip each stamen with a yellow dot and, using tweezers, place in the royal icing centre of the flowers while the icing is still wet. Prop with crumpled tissue paper. (Or buy artificial stamens.)

Almost any other flower can be copied and modelled in pastillage – orchids, daffodils and carnations can be made to look especially realistic.

A cake decorated with a Christmas rose, and trellis work.

A Christmas cake decorated with an attractively designed collar with lace insets.

The design and run-out work on this Christmas cake may be made as a whole collar, or as four sections with trellis bells to neaten the joins.

A Christmas cake decorated with six neat lace and run-out motifs placed together to form a collar. A bird neatens each join. A run-out figure decorates the top.

A Christmas cake decorated with a lace and run-out collar made in eight sections. The centre decoration is a run-out figure.

A Christmas cake decorated with a run-out scene, and a large run-out collar with open lace work.

A Christmas cake decorated with six open lace sections and an icing Christmas card.

A Christmas cake decorated with a collar which may be run-out as one collar, or made in sections.

A cake which features a large open work poinsettia and six lace work sections.

Run-out work

This type of work is also known as soft sugar or run-in (or flow-in) work. Although it is immensely popular for exhibition work, it is comparatively new for cake decorating at home. Cakes decorated with run-out look attractive and smart. It is suitable for carrying out almost any idea – a visit to a trade exhibition and a glimpse of the effects achieved in this particular branch of sugarcraft will fire anyone's ambition. With a little care, attractive decorations are produced and, though rather fragile for sale in shops, they are perfect for special occasion cakes. (See the picture on page 143 of a wedding cake with run-out butterflies.)

Equipment and materials required

The best material to work on is a piece of glass edged with sticky tape to prevent any accidents. Also necessary will be some waxed paper, greaseproof paper, a soft and a hard pencil, a soft good quality artist's paint brush, food colouring, a ruler and, if wished, a pair of compasses.

The method

The basic principle used in this work is to outline the shape required, and then to fill in the centre with soft royal icing. Begin by attempting small pieces of work until you are used to handling the delicate pieces and working this method. Then progress to larger run-outs. After a little practice, it is amazing how the large pieces stay intact in spite of handling.

To commence run-out work

As a start, try making small, round plaques, natural-sized flowers, or leaves; ivy leaves serve as a good beginning.

Find a suitably sized, well-shaped ivy leaf. Trace or copy the shape several times on to different pieces of smooth greaseproof paper – making all the leaves on one sheet of paper might result in breakages when they are removed. Using small dots of icing at each corner of the paper patterns, fasten down on to a sheet of glass. Cover each pattern with a square of waxed paper slightly larger than the greaseproof paper. Fasten with icing. Avoid allowing any icing under the actual tracing of the leaf.

Make some normal strength piping icing coloured light green; this is preferable to a dark green true ivy colour, as it is the idea that has to be conveyed rather than an actual copy. Outline the leaf pattern on waxed paper, using green royal icing and a No. 1 tube. There should be no breaks in the outline and it should be joined neatly at the points. Thin some of the icing in the basin with a little water or a little albumen solution, stirring the mixture carefully. Avoid beating as this makes air bubbles which are difficult to remove. The consistency should be similar to that of unwhipped double cream, just thick enough to coat the back of a spoon and the surplus from it to run back into the basin.

A cake covered with sugar paste and decorated with run-out ivy leaves.

Making run-out flowers.

Using a teaspoon, fill the leaf outline carefully, or put the icing into an icing bag, with the end cut to the equivalent to a No. 2 tube and fill the leaf from the bag, going round the outside first and gradually filling in the centre. This work should be carried out as quickly as possible, as the outer line should not be dry when the filling is put in, or it will show, and may break easily. Using a fine paint brush, move the icing round until the leaf is filled and no bubbles are showing. Any bubbles which do continue to rise must be pricked out with the brush or with a pin.

When completed, shake the sheet of glass gently and knock it lightly on the table to make sure that all the icing is quite even and level. The leaves should be full and rounded, but not so full that they are liable to overflow. If possible, place the sheet of leaves in front of an electric fire for a few seconds to set the surface, then dry in a warm, heated room overnight, or if possible for two or three days. When quite dry, store the leaves in an airtight container, still on the waxed paper, packed between layers of cotton wool.

To remove the ivy leaves from waxed paper
Place the leaf over the edge of a thick book and peel the waxed paper gently downwards. Turn the leaf round, loosening the points first, and then holding the leaf gently in one hand, continue bringing the waxed paper down and away from the leaf with the other.

Use ivy leaves with piped flowers as a flower arrangement in the centre or around the edge of a cake. As a finishing touch, pipe in a line to represent the vein of the leaf, and a line for the stem.

Run-out narcissi and daffodils
Draw the pattern for a narcissus or daffodil flower freehand, or take a tracing from a picture card or a catalogue. The flower should be positioned as if looking straight into the trumpet. Make the tracings each on to a separate piece of paper – about 12 should be sufficient for an 8-inch (20-cm.) cake. Fasten down on to a sheet of glass with dots of icing, and cover with waxed paper, also fastened with icing.

Pipe the outline of the flowers with a No. 1 or 0 tube, making sure not to go into the centre. Fill the flower with soft icing: yellow for daffodils and white for narcissi, running in the icing smoothly, using a paint brush to spread it evenly and remove any bubbles. The result will look like smooth icing. Leave to dry in a warm place.

After about 36 hours, and with a No. 0 tube in a bag filled with the same coloured icing, outline the outside edges of alternate petals only. When this is done, outline the entire edges of the

A two-tier cake decorated with the bishop's mitre, and flying angels on the edges of the cake. This cake was made for the consecration of a church.

A design taken from a school badge.

These heraldic designs would make excellent centrepieces for a boy's cake.

The separate sections ready to be placed on the top of the cake to make a three-dimensional picture (see page 152).

The completed three-dimensional cake.

remaining petals from the centres to the outside edges. This gives the effect of the three outer petals opening first, and being outside the three inner petals, as they are in reality. Inside the petals, make a neat circle of icing with a No. 0 tube. Continue working this circle two or three times, until the trumpet is long enough. On the last time round, flute the edge a little. Leave the flowers until quite dry, then paint the edge of the centre of narcissus trumpets with orange food colouring, using an artist's paint brush. The brush should be almost dry or else the colour may spread down the trumpet and spoil the effect. Look through a bulb catalogue to find different varieties, making daffodils with yellow petals and white centres, or yellow petals with orange centres. There are so many variations that it is almost impossible to go wrong.

To decorate a narcissus cake

These flowers are intricate to make, and for this reason perhaps best used on special occasion cakes. Arrange as a spray with a few piped leaves, or use around the edge of a cake as a flower border. When using a flower border pattern, half flowers should also be repeated on the board. Cut in half the original traced paper pattern, and place the tracing on the silver board to the edge of the completed cake. Outline in pencil on the board. Outline again, on top of the pencil line, using royal icing in a No. 1 or 0 tube. Fill the half flowers with soft icing, and leave to dry. Take care to fit in a complete number of flowers, and to take the icing to the edge of the cake.

Leave until quite dry and then pipe in the outline of the petals again, and half trumpets to match the full flowers. The half trumpets should be against the cake. Unless very great care is taken, the colour from yellow daffodils may seep up into the white icing on the cake. To cover this, fasten a narrow silver braid or ribbon just at the base of the cake with icing.

To complete a narcissus cake

Leave the completion of the top of the cake until last. Add any inscription or motif, and the half flowers around the base. Now, holding each flower carefully in the hand, draw off the waxed paper downwards, taking care not to force the paper or the flower may break. Turn the flower, loosening the edges of the petals first, and finally, the whole flower.

Make a rope of icing all around the top edge of the cake, using a star tube. Place the loose flowers on the rope, exactly above the half flowers on the board – the petals should fit in so well that the icing rope is hidden. Alternatively, a star of icing can be put on to the back of each flower. Whichever method is used, the flower should be raised a little and not lying flat. If necessary, add a series of stems, pull-out leaves or bought silver leaves between

A special occasion cake decorated with run-out narcissi.

each flower to neaten; if leaves are used towards the outside edge of the cake a similar row of leaves must be added to the flowers on the board, as they should be a reflection of the top row.

Marguerite daisies, yellow and orange marigolds, pink pyrethrums, pansies and other flat flowers can all be used in this way. The centre of the cake can be left plain, or hold greetings, a name, or a motif, but too much decoration can spoil a cake. Flowers are shown to their best advantage if the centre of the cake is left perfectly plain.

Wild roses

Trace a wild rose pattern from one of the cotton flowers sold in June on Alexandra Rose Day, a picture in a book, or draw one freehand. The best way to do this is to draw a circle the appropriate size, and to divide the circumference of the circle into five equal parts for the five petals. Make a dot in the centre of the circle and draw in the petals. Using very light pencil, divide the circle into five equal segments, joining the centre dot and the five points on the circumference. At the end of each division, make a small letter V, curved at the tops, and continue the curves, making a slight hollow in the centre of each petal. About 12 patterns will be needed for an 8-inch (20-cm) cake.

Cover the tracings with waxed paper and fasten down on glass.

Have ready some pale pink, rose coloured royal icing, and some thinned-out icing for the run-out work. Outline the petals of each flower at the edges only, not piping into the centres. Fill with the run-out icing and prick out any bubbles. Leave until dry, and then outline the petals almost to the middle with a No. 1 or 0 tube. Thin out the line of icing, pulling it off towards the centre of the flower. The two lines of each petal should lie together. Finish the centre with a circle of yellow dots, or fine lines thinning out from the centre to resemble rays. Experiment to find the most suitable effect.

To use these flowers as a decoration on a rich fruit cake, cut the pattern in half and use similarly to the narcissus design, placing the half-flowers around the base of the cake. Arrange touching each other, outlining with pencil and piping over the pencil line and filling in, as before, with thinned-out royal icing. When set, pipe over the outline again to form petals and fill in the yellow half-centre. If a pink tinge creeps up into the white icing, cover with a length of narrow silver braid or ribbon. Arrange the finished wild roses around the top of the cake, exactly above the half-flowers on the board, securing with a dab of icing. If liked, add an inscription in the centre of the cake.

Pansies

Make a tracing, using the same method as described in the making of a wild rose. Using yellow, white or pale mauve icing,

Run-out wild roses used to decorate a birthday cake. Half-flowers are used to decorate the bottom edge of the cake.

137

A three-dimensional cake with a fine collar with trellis insets.

Two examples of three-dimensional work. The paper pattern is used as a guide for the run-out collar.

Run-out pansies can be made following the instructions for making wild roses. They make attractive decorations around the top and base of a cake covered with either royal icing or sugar paste.

When making run-out lilies, place the run-out icing (before it dries) over a rolling pin so that each petal is curved.

outline the lower large petal in each flower on to waxed paper, fill with thinned-out royal icing, and leave to dry. When set, outline the two upper petals and fill with deeper yellow, deeper mauve or white. When these are dry, complete one more petal on one side, and the final petal on the opposite side of the flower. By outlining and completing each petal separately, a distinctive effect is achieved, and two colours or shades can be put into the same flower.

To complete, when the icing is dry, paint the pansy face in streaks with food colouring using a fine brush. Centre the flower with an elongated dot of green. Use in flower arrangements, or around the top and base of a cake on a surface of royal icing or sugar paste. Glacé icing is not suitable for use with these flowers, as the soft icing makes the flowers run.

Lilies

A curved piece of run-out is needed to make a good lily. Draw a suitably sized circle, divide into eight sections, and from this basic pattern make eight petals. Using the tracing, run-out these petals flat on to waxed paper, and then before the icing is dry place them over a rolling pin or a rounded tin to make a convex petal. For a concave petal, place the run-out in a basin or a hollow round. Hold near a source of heat and rotate backwards and forwards for a few minutes until the surface of the icing is set. Leave for a day or two to become quite firm, then place in position on the cake, making a firm star of icing under the central point of the flower where all the petals meet. Prop in position with cotton wool or tissue paper until quite set.

This decoration is suitable for the centre of the top tier of a wedding or for a christening cake – a tiny doll can be placed in the centre of the flower, if it is made large enough.

Run-out rings

Rings can be made similarly to lily petals by placing an oblong strip of run-out icing three-quarters of the way around a suitably sized stick, making sure that the icing is slack enough to be removed when set. For safety, use double waxed paper, as most run-outs are liable to make the waxed paper soft and stick to the mould.

Make lace strips or lace centres with run-out edges in the same way, flat on waxed paper, and quickly, while still soft, place around the curved surface. Alternatively, work the lace on a greased surface, perhaps a serviette ring, and warm the ring over a source of heat to remove the icing.

Place these run-out rings on the edge of an iced cake as if biting into the edge of the cake.

See the picture, on page 59, of a Christmas cake with run-out rings around the top edge.

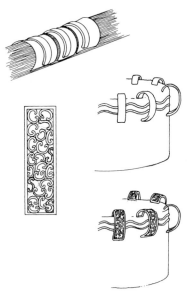

Run-out rings, made with or without lace centres, make an attractive decoration for the top edge of an iced cake.

Run-out figures. Each section is run in separately and then allowed to set to make the divisions for the clothes, arms and legs.

Blossom petals

Use tiny heart shapes or pointed ovals, similar to lily petals. Have ready a suitably curved hollow tin or saucer, and two batches of icing – thinned-out royal icing in pink and white, and some softer than usual line piping icing. Make sure that the mould is well greased.

Pipe single petals on to separate pieces of waxed paper, place immediately into the mould and, using a brush, fill with white thinned-out icing. With a second brush, fill in the base of the petal with pink soft icing. Take great care, as each petal should be thin and delicate. When all the petals are dry, store in an airtight container until needed.

To assemble on the cake, pipe a branch in brown icing on the dry cake surface, place the petals in position with tweezers, securing with a dot of icing piped on the cake. Prop with tissue paper until dry. Finish the spray with green pull-out leaves, iced straight on to the branch. Pipe in stamens, or arrange previously made ones while the centre is still wet.

Use petals to represent apple, peach, cherry, hawthorn, lilac or any other blossom, according to size, colour and shape.

To pipe run-out figures

This method of icing run-outs can be used for producing all kinds of figures: animals, children skating, children dancing and skipping, nursery rhyme characters or ballet dancers. There is no end to the list of possibilities. The figure can be run out whole and then painted, or it can be run out in sections, forming divisions between clothing and limbs. One layer of icing can be run out on top of another, giving the effect of folds and thicknesses.

Swans *Illustrated on page 175*

Learning how to make run-out swans is the next step in progression through this branch of cake decoration. Begin in the accepted way, by drawing a swan, or taking a tracing from a picture. The two wings should be made separately from the body and head of the bird. Following the same method used to make an ivy leaf (see page 132), outline the swan, and the left and right wings by piping on to waxed paper. Fill with soft icing. Prick out the bubbles and leave to dry.

When the body of the swan is quite dry, turn it over and outline again on the actual icing. Fill in with soft icing. This step should not be repeated for the wings. Leave on waxed paper to dry and in the meantime, using a No. 1 or 0 tube, pipe in lines on the wings to represent feathers, working up towards the tail, leaving the breast ends of the wings quite smooth. Rub with the fingers to accentuate this smoothness.

When the body and head are quite dry, colour the beak with orange food colouring and put in the black seer with confec-

A square white royal iced wedding cake decorated with pink roses and braided panels.

A beautifully decorated two-tier wedding cake. Run-out butterflies are placed around the edges; trellis and braiding form the main patterns on the cakes.

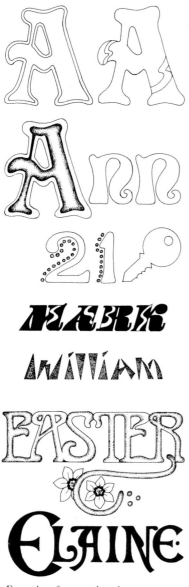

Examples of run-out lettering.

tioner's black, a mixture of blue, red and brown food colouring, or a soft graphite pencil. Notice by studying a good picture of a swan, that this black marking is quite large and the eye is almost a continuation. When the head is completed, make a bulb of icing each side of the body and place the wings in position. Prop with tissue paper until set. To make curved wings, work the icing on a greased hard-boiled egg or on the side of a rounded can.

Sugarcraft theatre scenes

If you are ambitious it is possible to produce a whole sugarcraft theatre, scenery and figures. To accentuate the folds in the clothing or various parts of the scenery sections, outline one section at a time and fill with run-out icing and allow to dry before putting in the next section near which may be a different colour of icing.

To speed up the work, sections which do not lie together or touch each other may be completed at the same time. Using coloured icing helps here but for real effect shading must be done with food colouring diluted with water and an artist's fine brush.

This is very absorbing work although it is time consuming, but much satisfaction can be gained when a piece has been completed for a special occasion. Some parts of the clothing on the figures can be decorated with edible glitter (see page 164). See page 188 for drawings of figures.

Run-out sugar letters and figures

Make drawings of the required letters or numbers – these can be traced from books or cards. Fasten the figure down on a sheet of glass. Cover with waxed paper and outline in full strength royal icing and a No. 1 tube. Run in the soft icing (if to be used lying flat) on one side then on the second side – if the letter or figure is to stand upright. When quite dry these letters or figures can be arranged standing on a star of icing on the cake. If you want an outline of coloured icing, the letter should first be outlined in colour and allowed to dry before the run-out sugar in another colour is used. When dry, the letters and figures can be decorated daintily with a fine trailing stem and minute roses or forget-me-nots and green leaves; or edged with picot dots of full strength royal icing to give a lacy effect.

Chinese-type letters and fancy-shaped letters are very successful in run-out sugar.

Advanced run-out work

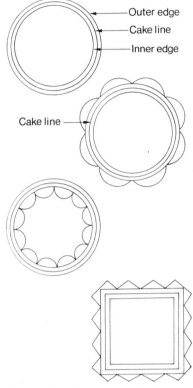

Outer edge
Cake line
Inner edge

Cake line

Patterns for making run-out circular or square collars for special occasion cakes.

An Easter cake decorated with a run-out collar with scalloped edges.

The scope of run-out work extends far beyond the decorations described in the previous chapter. This method can also be used to make an attractively shaped collar to surround a simple cake, and lift it from the ordinary to the special, giving it a finished, tailor-made look.

To make a large circular or square run-out collar

Great care must be taken when making large run-outs. They are liable to break easily, and yet with a little care, it is amazing how much handling they will withstand. A run-out collar gives an excellent finish to a cake and tends to make a small cake look larger. A round cake should have a round collar and a square cake a square collar, but to give an unusual design it is possible to put a square collar on a round cake or vice versa.

The silver cake drum or thick board should be about 4 inches (10 cm.) larger than the cake, according to the size of the run-out being used. This acts as a protection against breakages and adds to the appearance of the cake.

Measure the size of the cake with a ruler or tape measure. Making sure to leave a margin all round, draw the exact shape of the cake top on to a sheet of greaseproof paper. It is possible to take measurements from the cake tin, but if thick layers of almond paste and icing have been added, these must be taken into account. From now on, the pencilled outline of the cake will be called the cake line. It may be helpful to write these words along this original line, to save any mistakes.

Outline the shape of the cake twice more, once on the outside and once on the inside of the cake line, making both lines $\frac{1}{2}$ inch (1 cm.) from the cake line. This is all the pattern that is required to make a plain collar. To add a scalloped edge, use a pair of compasses to draw the scallops around the outer circle, or use the folding paper method. For a large scallop design, or a deep bracket shape, the inner edge may be allowed slightly inside the $\frac{1}{2}$ inch (1 cm.). Alternatively, scallops may also be put on the inside of the collar.

When the pattern is completed, cut it out with scissors and fit it over the cake to see if the whole effect is suitable and well-balanced. For good support the collar should over-lap the edge of the cake inside by $\frac{1}{2}$ inch (1 cm.) all the way around.

Make a new perfectly smooth, clean pattern on fresh grease-proof paper by drawing round the original pattern (keep the pattern for use later on). Do not cut out the new pattern, as the edges can be used to fasten on to the glass with a dab of icing, or with drawing pins on to a board. A large board or glass will be needed to make this large run-out – preferably glass, as it remains perfectly flat and does not absorb the liquid from the icing. Make absolutely sure that there is no icing and there are no drawing pins under the pattern of the actual collar. Cover tightly with thin,

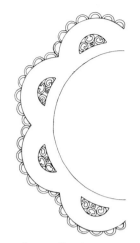

A pattern for a scalloped collar with lace insets.

A cake decorated with a more elaborate collar.

smooth waxed paper fastened down with icing at the corners.

Make the soft sugar or run-out icing by adding a little water or albumen solution to some well beaten, normal strength royal icing until it is the consistency of unwhipped double cream. Do not beat when adding the liquid. Stir gently but thoroughly, scraping down any thick icing from the spoon or the sides of the basin so that the consistency is perfectly even. About 8 tablespoons soft icing is sufficient for an 8-inch (20-cm.) run-out collar. Be careful to make enough icing before beginning the collar, as it dries quickly and any join will show. Left-over soft icing can always be added to the original and re-beaten, adding more sugar if necessary, and perhaps a little more albumen to bring it up to strength. When the run-out icing is made, cover with a cloth and leave for a few minutes until the bubbles subside.

While the icing is standing, outline the design with piping strength icing and a No. 1 tube. Break at any points in the design and join again neatly, avoiding joins in a circular scallop. It is not easy to pipe all the way around the inner circle with only the one finishing join, but with practice and experience, and by lifting the icing slightly, it will soon become possible. While the soft outer line is still wet stir the run-out icing gently and then fill in the pattern with this icing, using a teaspoon, or piping it from a bag with a hole cut to the size equivalent to a No. 2 tube. Work around the edge of the design first, so that it cannot become dry (a dried edge will show a line). For the same reason, work from each side of a large collar, so that the icing cannot dry in a ridge.

Use a fine brush for spreading the icing and removing any bubbles. When the collar is finished, prick out any remaining bubbles, gently lift the sheet of glass and knock it gently on the table. This should level the icing. Again, prick out any bubbles that may have appeared and leave the collar quite undisturbed for two or three days until completely dry. If you place it about 2 feet (62 cm.) away from a warm electric fire for a few minutes this should produce an attractive gloss.

One of the best places for drying these run-outs is a slightly heated airing cupboard, although the icing must not be left in this atmosphere for too long, or it will become yellow and discoloured. When the run-out is nearly dry and there is no risk of stickiness, protect it from the dust with a light covering of tissue paper.

To complete the decoration on a run-out collar

Outlining the collar with over-piping will give a bolder effect and add strength, but for pure decoration add a simple lace work edge of dots or tiny lines – this will also camouflage a bad edge. Decoration can be added in colour, although this is only for the more advanced student. White icing is less likely to show defects. This work is done while the collar is on waxed paper on glass.

Run-out and lace work combined to decorate the corners of a square cake.

Variations on the plain run-out collar

As an alternative to the collars already described, cut-out spaces can be left and filled in with net work similar to the trellis and lace work described on pages 109 and 112. For a 21st cake, the number 21 can be incorporated in the run-out, or perhaps some initials. These must first be planned in the original pattern, drawn carefully to scale and outlined at the same time as the collar itself. In this case, use the soft icing in a bag for filling, as it is difficult to flood the small spaces between the letters, and if the edge line breaks, the whole design will probably have to be started all over again.

To put the run-out pattern on to the board

When the cake is made and completed with a good dry surface, a reflection of the run-out collar pattern should be made on the cake board around the base of the cake.

Take the first paper pattern made and cut along the cake line. Cut the pattern in half and place the two halves to meet around the base of the cake, if necessary cutting a little more paper away to ensure a good fit. Fasten down lightly with a little icing. Pencil round the pattern and remove the paper.

Using piping icing and a No. 1 tube, pipe around the outline slightly on the outer side, so that no pencil mark can be seen when the design is filled. Have the soft sugar ready and fill in the space between the outline and the cake. If there are no cut-out spaces use a teaspoon to fill the space and spread with an artist's fine brush to remove any bubbles. For a design with spaces, use a piping bag to fill in the soft sugar. Make sure that the icing flows neatly to the base of the cake, particularly if coloured run-out is being used. Any lace work should be done before the soft sugar is put in.

When the board work is dry, complete the picot edge, and any other decoration (except standing ornaments) to the cake. If necessary, add a silver braid or decorative ribbon.

To remove the collar from the waxed paper

This is very difficult and often leads to disappointment. The only approach is to be pleased when the collar comes off intact, rather than despondent when it breaks. Any arrangements of previously piped flowers should be put on to the collar before it is removed from the waxed paper, making sure that all the decoration is firmly attached to the icing collar.

Place the run-out to the edge of a table or flat upturned tray, and very carefully peel off the waxed paper downwards. Turn the collar frequently, loosening around the edges first and then gradually working to the middle. When the entire collar is quite loose, work any picot dots to correspond with the collar on the board; when quite dry, re-loosen the run-out. Some of the picot

147

edge may break off, but can be replaced either immediately, or when the collar is on the cake. If a trellis or lines are planned for behind the collar, turn it over very carefully and, using a stiff icing, pipe in the trellis lines right across the back over the shortest edges of the cut-outs. The lines should be taut and not sagging. For this reason work the trellis the shortest distance across the open cut-out. Complete the trellis, at right angles to the first lines, and allow to dry before turning the collar over to place it on the cake.

To fasten the collar to the top of the cake, make a rope of icing with a No. 5 star tube right around the edge of the cake. While the rope is still wet, carefully lift the loosened run-out from the waxed paper and place in position with the pattern exactly corresponding to the collar round the base of the cake. The collar should be a little raised from the cake, and not flat on the iced surface.

Sometimes a silver braid is put around the top of the cake before putting on the rope of icing to hold the collar. This neatens the edge and is a support for the collar.

To complete the cake

Add any final decorations – swans, ballet dancers, animals, etc., and prop in position with tissue paper until the icing fixing them to the cake surface is quite firm and dry. A fine silver braid can be used to tidy the cake between the base and the run-out sugar, especially if the white icing is tinged from a coloured run-out. If preferred pipe small scrolls or stars. This is best done before putting the top collar on the cake.

If the collar becomes broken in two or three places, it can be pieced together with a little icing. When quite dry, these joins can be disguised with a piped flower or fern. This will not pass in examination work, but it can still look attractive for home purposes.

Smaller sections of run-out work

A large run-out design can be cut into small sections, made as individual pieces and assembled on the cake top to form a complete run-out design. Rectangular pieces can be placed alternatively with lacy patterns or flowers. This looks particularly effective, and the pieces are far easier to handle, also easier to replace if a breakage does occur. Fasten them with a small dot of icing.

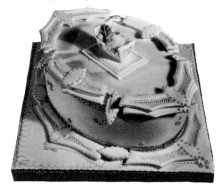

An oval Christening cake decorated with pieces of run-out work.

The combination of lace work and run-out work

A cake decorated with a carefully made lace and run-out collar.

There is something doubly fascinating when these two forms of sugarcraft are used in the same piece of work. It is essential to design the basic shape of the pattern with some solid and some lacy work before beginning the actual icing. The lace work need not be the same pattern throughout. Even on one small section of the design, the lace pattern can be varied. This is what makes the combination of lace and run-out work so dainty and exciting.

Prepare this work in the usual way, fixing the greaseproof paper pattern on to a sheet of glass and covering with waxed paper. Firstly, outline the design, secondly fill in the lace work, and finally run in the soft sugar work, using a fine paint brush or a bag (a teaspoon may hold too much and overflow the icing on to the lace work).

A square cake with roses

Begin in the usual way by drawing the pattern on greaseproof paper, copying the design from the picture. Fasten down each section on a sheet of glass and cover with thin waxed paper. Make each section on a separate piece of waxed paper, or there will be a danger of breakage when the pieces of icing are removed. Make several extra sections so that no time is wasted while replacements dry.

Using a No. 1 tube, outline the pattern and then make the lace work, filling in with the letter 'x' in the centre and loops in the side. Finally, run in the soft sugar icing, completing each section before beginning work on the next.

While these sections are drying, make sure that the cake and board are completed. The surface of the cake should be perfectly finished and the board should be 4 inches (10 cm.) wider on all sides than the actual cake. Cut out the main outlines of the pattern and trace on to the board. Work similarly to the top sections and fill in the soft sugar work close up to the edge of the cake and around the edge of the design. When dry, outline with a fine tube and add several dots to give a finish to the centre of the soft sugar edging. When examining these pictures a magnifying glass may be useful.

While the board work is drying, pipe some bells on a well greased metal bell mould and, when dry, remove by holding in front of a source of heat and easing off very carefully as the grease melts. Place on cotton wool until needed. Tie four strips of silver ribbon into four bows and place at the lower corners held in place with stiff icing. Fix the bells near the ribbon, two at each corner, resting on the board, again using icing to secure in place.

To fix the top lace sections Although these lace pieces have wide run-out work on the inside edges to attach them to the cake, it is still necessary to hold them in position until quite dry. Pile some books or a similar substitute, to the correct height of the corners of the cake, and on top of the pile place a ruler against the

A square wedding cake decorated with two patterns of lace work and white pastillage roses.

edge of the cake. This supports the lace work until it is set firmly in place. Run a line of icing along the edge of the cake, and after removing the waxed paper, place one of the lace work sections in place and at the same time, set the opposite section in place. Leave the cake undisturbed with both sections set in place in a warm room for two or three days until completely dry. Draw the books away carefully, one at a time, perhaps removing one jutting out from the pile first. Very great care must be taken, as the least vibration will shake the lace work and break it. Repeat exactly the same procedure to fix the remaining two lace sections in place.

To complete the cake Make four birds and place one at each top corner, centering the cake with three large pastillage roses and a few silver leaves. This design is suitable for a three-tier wedding cake or for a 21st birthday cake, with a suitable inscription and lace work 21, standing in the centre. It is not generally satisfactory for transporting any great distance, although if this is absolutely necessary, settle the cake on the floor of a car on several cushions to take any vibration, then it can be safely and carefully taken on a short journey.

Double run-outs

This method is a combination of large, plain run-out and lace. Complete the large run-out first on waxed paper, and the reflection around the cake on the board. Make lace or lace and soft sugar pieces to follow the outer line of the plain run-out shape. Plan similar pieces, or simply plain run-outs for the board. Fix the pieces in position with hidden stars of icing. Before fixing any of the top run-outs in place, complete any other decorations or writing to avoid the slightest chance of breaking the fragile lace work.

The welcome cake

This cake has a first layer of plain run-out – and four cut-out semi-circles filled in with trellis on the back. Top the plain sections which have not been cut out with a second piece of run-out and lace work following exactly the same basic design; fill the centre with a lacy pattern. In this picture, the letters of welcome have been outlined in pale pink sugar and then run in straight on to the surface of the cake, using pale pink soft sugar icing (this is known as relief work): these may be made in advance on waxed paper and then placed in position. This method is preferable for dark coloured letters, as they may run into the white icing if outlined and run in straight on to the cake surface.

A 'Welcome' cake decorated with a plain collar with small lace insets and extra raised pieces.

Add a spray of anemones and a sprig of fern to complete the surface of the cake. More anemones may be placed around the base of the cake. (Make the anemones from almond paste coloured red and purple with food colouring.) Finally, fix a piece of silver braid around the cake.

A wedding cake decorated with complete double run-outs.

Complete double run-outs

The picture opposite shows a wedding cake using whole double run-outs. Place a plain shaped run-out on the cake first, and then cover it with a lacy section exactly the same shape and size as the original run-out, with a large bell let into the work. Fix the two run-outs with several tall stars, raising the top one a little from the first plain one underneath. Join the edges with a loop pattern. Run-out the initials on waxed paper and when dry place on the cake, using a slight raising star.

A template should be cut to make the dainty hanging loop design on the side of the cake. This must always be completed before putting the main run-outs in place.

Run-outs raised from the board *Illustrated on page 95*

Sometimes it is useful to be able to raise the bottom run-out next to the board by $\frac{1}{2}$ inch (1 cm.) or so. For this, the run-out should be made on waxed paper as before, but the diameter of the centre circle should be $\frac{1}{2}$ inch (1 cm.) larger, as the whole run-out has to be placed over the cake, before it can be fixed in position; check the size of the cake. Place several large stars on the board, about $\frac{1}{2}$ inch (1 cm.) from the side of the cake, and leave to set. These will support the run-out circle. When dry, place second stars alternately between the first stars and, while still wet, lower the dry run-out circle very carefully over the cake and into position. Make sure it is level and then leave to set firmly in place. Neaten by filling in the $\frac{1}{4}$-inch ($\frac{1}{2}$-cm.) space between the cake and circle with a row of icing stars or beads.

Raising this run-out collar above the board allows icicles to be put on the edge. For further ideas and designs look at the pictures of cakes on pages 162, 166 and 167, combining lace work and run-out work.

A birthday cake decorated in the centre with a run-out and sugar lace doily.

151

Three-dimensional work and heraldry

A three-dimensional cake showing a lakeland scene.

The pictures on pages 135, 138 and 139, showing three-dimensional work, hardly do justice to the effect that can be created. There is no difficulty for the artist to draw a picture of a local view and set out the design for a three-dimensional iced cake. The majority of readers will have to look for a picture in a magazine or choose a suitable card from which to copy. A view is a standard idea to choose, one with mountains in the background, a church or house in the centre with trees and a lake, river or fence in the foreground. With perhaps one or two people or an animal near the front.

First examine the chosen picture and decide what part can be put on the iced cake surface. (The pictures on page 135 have been chosen to illustrate how to work the 3-D picture.) Next cut three pieces of greaseproof paper the size and shape of the cake top. Decide which is to be the horizon and draw or trace the horizon or sky line on one piece of greaseproof paper. Draw any trees near, above or just below the line and take the line round the top of the houses and the hillside and draw in any stones, grass and fences. Also draw in the line for the river. On the next paper take a lower line in the foreground including the Christmas tree on the left and the people on the bridge, along the line of the top of the bridge and the other four evergreen trees. Mark in the line where the river banks are. On the third paper take a tracing of the snowman and the land on which he is standing. Each horizon line must extend to the edge of the circle of paper and each paper must have a tracing of what would appear on the picture a little below the next section.

Place all the three papers over each other to get an idea of the balance of the picture. On the snowman paper draw out a few extra trees and people perhaps choosing figures from another card if wished as these may help to improve the final result. Next place each paper on a sheet of glass and fasten down with a few dots of icing near the top so they are not near the run-out. Cover with separate pieces of waxed paper. With white royal icing and No. 1 tube, outline the tracing line in the first pattern – the sky line of the hill and the houses and right round to the lower edge to make a continuous line not any tracing in the centre of the sheet. Flood with the soft run-out icing. In the same way outline the traced foreground line of the second section leaving open the part over the river and continuing round the lower edge of the paper. Repeat with the snowman figure, any extra trees or figures and flood as required to make a third section. The result will be rather unusual in appearance but when completed the picture will soon take shape. Leave to dry for two or three days in a warm, airy place. Now outline the tracing on the reverse side with a soft pencil using only the necessary detail. Place the tracings in their respective positions on the dry icing run-out and retrace the picture using a black lead or graphite pencil. Press only lightly so the sheet of icing will not be broken. Trace only the necessary detail, a feint line will show on the icing which may be outlined again if wished. Using food colouring diluted to the right shade with water, and an artist's fine brush (a saucer is good to use for mixing and diluting the colours), first paint in the sky with very pale blues and perhaps green and some pale pink or yellow and the hills on the cake itself. Use only very little liquid on the brush as the base being painted is sugar and this tends to melt. When dry add any trees or flying birds, as wished. They may all be traced from the original picture on to the cake top if wished.

Now paint the run-out sugar sections following the tracing and consult the original picture for detail and shading. Even the less artistic readers can achieve a result which is surprising when the cake is put together later. Do not worry about the result at this stage, but remember to keep all the colour pale and dainty.

To complete the 3-D picture When all the sections are dry, pipe a rope of royal icing with a star tube all around the top of the cake and one or two stars in the centre and place the first and largest section in position below the sky painted on the cake. Wait for the rope of icing to become quite firm before putting a second rope all the way around the cake and one or two stars to prop the next section of the run-out. Place the second run-out piece in position, the first having been painted to just below the line where the house top comes. Allow to dry for a while before a third rope of icing and the final run-out is put in place. Consider the whole picture and tidy up where necessary with icing. A little piping of royal icing using a fine tube only may help in adding touches of snow or roots at the base of a tree, or extra leaves in the foreground and place in any extra figures required. Figures of people and trunks of trees can be outlined and flooded lightly to give a rounded effect. These bits may be painted in later or coloured icing used where suitable. Try to keep the rope wall of icing very neat as it may show when the cake is finished.

Complete any icing required on the board under the cake and have ready a suitable collar quite firm and dry to give a frame to the picture. Naturally, this fascinating work is for special occasions.

A three-dimensional cake showing a Christmas scene.

Heraldry and other figures
Family crests, coats of arms, school badges or shields can all be represented in run-out sugar and make an excellent centrepiece for a cake for a suitable occasion. The details of this figure must of necessity be correct in shape and colours but the size can be made larger or smaller to fit the position where it is to be put on the cake.

Make a drawing of the badge the size required, or it may be possible to take a tracing. Then make small tracings of each section. Place all the piece on glass and cover with waxed paper. Outline the sections in colour and fill in with coloured run-out icing. Leave until quite set and firm and then assemble with a dot of royal icing under each piece. Work in any detail still required with a No. 00 tube and slightly softer icing than the run-out icing. (See the pictures on page 134.)

This excellent work is fine for making delightful Christmas and birthday cards or calendars, as special gifts.

Make some oblong run-out pieces in the usual way in white or colour and leave to dry. Trace choir boys from old Christmas cards, calendars or pictures. Make run-out copies of these. When dry, paint the figures with food colouring and when dry mount on the already dry run-out base.

A superb cake showing an old car on a cake top with Santa Claus and the Christmas tree is on page 131. A seasonal greeting can be written on cards using an artist's fine brush, or an architect's pen filled with food colouring. Any of these cards or figures only, can be used as a centrepiece for the top of a cake to suit the occasion. They should be made well in advance and stored on cotton wool in an airtight tin.

A cake for a music enthusiast with a record and plaques of composers names and a choir boy, can be seen in the picture on page 107.

Finally, touch in extra details with food colouring and a fine brush. Gold powder mixed with a little gin may be used in small quantities for gilding. This is generally considered safe although it is meant only as a decoration and should not be eaten in large quantities. Final lines can be added and emphasised where necessary with over-piping with a No. 00 tube.

If these badges and figures are required to stand upright on a cake, both sides should be completed in detail. To do this, outline the back of a badge or figure, around the edge, with a No. 1 tube and royal icing. Fill with run-out soft sugar and when dry repeat the details from the front of the badge, so that it looks attractive seen from any angle. If the figure of a person is made to stand, the back view of the person should be made – not two faces. With this in mind it is useful to be able to make a figure with a profile. (See the picture on page 162 showing the dancing ladies on a 21st birthday Wedgwood cake.)

A coat of arms. Each section of this was run out separately and mounted on the background.

To make
and design
cake models

A cake modelled to represent a specific house or church always provokes delight and admiration. It is interesting to work, and a very personal gift to receive. Model cakes can be made to represent almost anything: a particular house or garden, windmills, prams, fairytale coaches and crinoline lady cakes all prove popular for special occasion cakes. Even a model village may be made – see the picture on page 90.

To make a cake model
Use a Madeira or fruit cake mixture, and bake it in a square or oblong tin, depending on the shape of the model, the occasion, and the amount of work to be put on to the cake. Do not hollow out the centre of the cake mixture before baking, as the baked cake should be slightly domed. If the cake does not rise, cut a piece from the side to build up the top into a roof shape; use jam to fix the pieces into position and a piece of almond paste to fill in the spaces between the cake sections.

Aim at a well-shaped roof on a model house or shop. A church or other more complicated models may have to be made in two or three pieces and put together after being partly decorated.

The covering A variety of mixtures may be used to cover the outside of model cakes – almond paste, sugar paste, run-out icing pieces, or even pastillage, which gives a good appearance and, although rather hard for general use, is readily eaten by children.

Royal icing may be used for piping structural decorations, and flowers and trees in the garden. Pressed maidenhair and asparagus fern can be used for trees with icing trunks, and green coconut can be spread on royal icing to represent grass. Use coloured sugar for paths and soil, and brown sugar for sand. If necessary, pieces of rustless wire covered with icing may be used to give strength to trees, bridges, gateways and arches.

To begin the model Make sure that the cake is on a board large enough to hold the planned garden. Measure the cake carefully and make a paper pattern the exact size of the outside of the house. Lay the pattern on rolled out sugar or almond paste, and cut out the pieces with a sharp knife. Scissors will be useful for trimming. Coat the paste thinly with apricot jam and place on the cake, arranging the pieces neatly, pressing well into position and making neat joins at the corners of walls and roofs. Leave to dry.

Meanwhile cover the roof with a layer of almond paste, like the walls, especially if it has been built up from pieces of cake, and then cut circles of coloured paste which can be arranged overlapping, beginning at the lower edge. Arrange a paste chimney, and model any pieces needed for the garden – steps, figures – or for the house – doors and shutters for the windows. Alternatively, run-out pieces of icing can be made the correct size to represent the walls of the house, and fixed on the cake with royal icing. Pastillage may also be used for the roof as it holds its shape well.

A church modelled from sugar paste.

To pipe in the details With royal icing, pipe in windows, doors, strands of straw for a thatched roof, crazy paving etc. Often a picture is useful at this stage. Spread the board with thin royal icing, bringing it right up to the model. Sprinkle with green coconut to represent grass. Pipe in flower beds, filling them with dark brown sugar to represent the soil. Place flowers, piped beforehand, into position in the garden.

Animals, motor cars and people can be modelled in sugar paste and fixed in position with a bulb of icing. Prop them until dry and firm. Let the imagination run riot in building up these models – the more detail, the greater the children's delight. If possible, let older children help to make them, developing their sense of achievement and creative self-expression.

Flat models

Decide on the shape of the model, and then make a paper pattern. Musical instruments – violin, banjo, double bass – are easy to model and good for a musical party.

Bake a Madeira cake mixture in a large, flat roasting tin. If the model is large, two cakes may be needed.

Using the paper pattern, cut the cake to shape, fixing any joins together with apricot jam.

Roll out some almond paste, cut it to shape and spread with jam. Place it on the top and sides of the cake. Place on an oblong silver board and pipe in strings, pegs, and any other details, first making sure that these details are correct and accurate.

Figures

The best ingredients for modelling are sugar paste, and almond paste with a little extra icing sugar added. Storks, cradles, and other white ornaments for christening and wedding cakes can be made from pastillage 1, but generally this is not the best ingredient to use as it hardens too quickly, and any modelling has to be carried out simply, accurately and at speed. It is better to use modelling fondant or pastillage 2 or 3.

Some people are born with a natural gift for modelling figures. Even so, this is something that anyone, with patience, can learn to do. Try first to make the bodies of the figures in the right proportion. Then, choosing the most suitable tools to hand – knife, skewer, pin, etc. – put in the details. With care and time, realistic, exciting results can come simply from studying a picture or, better still, a real life subject.

A musical instrument cake.

Wedding and other special occasion cakes

On birthdays, at Christmas and Easter time, and when a couple announce their engagement are all times when the cake decorator and the unusual and decorative cake come into their own. But chief among all these special occasion cakes is the cake that is made for a wedding.

To make a wedding cake
The cake tin Use square, round, heart-shaped or horseshoe-shaped tins, varying each tier in size, taking, as a rough guide, three round tins 10 (26), 8 (20) and 6 inches (15 cm.), 11 (28), 9 (23) and 7 inches (18 cm.), or even 12 (30), 9 (23) and 6 inches (15 cm.) in diameter. However, it is most usual to have a difference of 2 inches (5 cm.) between each tier.

Line the tin with double greaseproof paper and tie a double band of brown paper around the outside. Place on a baking tray with a layer of salt, sand or cardboard underneath to save direct heat contacting the cake. Make sure that the baking tray is not tight to the sides of the oven as the heat must be able to circulate freely around the cake. Horseshoe- and number-shaped cakes often have no base, in which case it is advisable to place the tin on two baking trays if possible.

To bake the cakes Always use the centre of the oven, and never bake more than one cake at a time unless the centre shelf is large enough to take the two tins at once. Some domestic ovens are not deep enough to take a cake with a diameter of 12 inches (30 cm.). In this case, a 10-inch (26-cm.) cake will have to be the bottom tier, with upper tiers of 8 (20) and 6 inches (15 cm.), or 7 (18) and 4 inches (10 cm.).

Always allow the oven to heat to the correct temperature before putting in the cake.

To calculate the correct quantities The following recipe is sufficient for an 8-inch (20-cm.) round tin, making a cake 3 inches ($7\frac{1}{2}$ cm.) deep. For a 10-inch (26-cm.) tin, use one and a half times the quantities given. For a 6-inch (15-cm.) tin, halve the quantities. For a square cake, use one and a quarter times each quantity.

As the higher tiers of a wedding cake become smaller, so the depth should decrease correspondingly. This gives good proportion to the cake, which otherwise would look top heavy. If, after baking, the cake is still not the correct depth, cut down, or build up with almond paste, to produce the correct balance. Level the top of a cake if it has risen in the centre, or if the depth of the cake will not allow for cutting, build up the edges with extra almond paste, until the surface is flat. The top of a wedding cake must always be perfectly flat.

Baking time The baking time given in this recipe is for an 8-inch (20-cm.) middle-sized cake. Bake 1 hour more for the largest, and 1 hour less for the smallest. The temperature is the same for all sizes.

A two-tier wedding cake decorated with white pastillage roses.

157

Wedding cake

IMPERIAL/METRIC

8 oz./225 g. butter
8 oz./225 g. brown sugar
4 large eggs
10 oz./275 g. plain flour
2 oz./50 g. ground almonds
pinch salt
2 teaspoons black treacle
1 teaspoon mixed spice
1 teaspoon instant coffee powder
1 teaspoon cocoa powder
grated rind of 1 orange and 1
    lemon
8 oz./225 g. currants
8 oz./225 g. raisins
8 oz./225 g. Valencia raisins,
    stoned
8 oz./225 g. sultanas
2 oz./50 g. candied peel
2 oz./50 g. glacé cherries

Cooking time: 4½–6 hours
Oven temperature: cool
(275°F., 140°C., Gas Mark 1)
Makes: one 8-inch (20-cm.)
cake

Wash and dry all fruit the day before mixing the cake. Have the 8-inch (20-cm.) round tin prepared, lined with two sheets of greaseproof paper and with double brown paper tied around the outside.

Cream the butter and sugar until very light. Add the eggs, one at a time, one teaspoon flour, the ground almonds, salt, treacle, spice, coffee and cocoa powders, orange and lemon rinds. Mix well. Fold in the flour, adding the fruit and peel, and the cherries, tossed in a little flour. Mix thoroughly and put into the lined tin. Place the cake on a baking tray in the centre of the preheated oven and cook for 4½–6 hours. This long, slow cooking gives a good, rich, dark colour.

When cooked, allow to cool in the tin for about 10 minutes, and then turn out on to a wire rack. When cold, wrap in greaseproof paper and put into a tin. If there is no suitable tin, wrap the cake in foil. Keep for 3–4 weeks before icing. When the cake is about a week old, prick the top in several places with a skewer and pour a little spirit (rum or brandy) over the cake from a teaspoon. Make sure there is not too much spirit to be absorbed into the small holes, as the cake should not be made wet. Wrap up again afterwards in the greaseproof paper and foil.

Cover the top and sides with almond paste, using the recipe on page 33 and following the instructions on that page.

To cover the cake with royal icing
Royal icing is used for wedding cakes. Put 3 egg whites (or albumen substitute) into a bowl and add 1 lb. (450 g.) icing sugar and make royal icing to coat the cake. It is impossible to make exactly the right amount of icing, with none left over, as there must be sufficient to cover the cake and then to scrape off smoothly leaving a good surface.

Following the method described on page 46, begin by icing the largest cake first, making sure to wipe the silver board clean after each layer of icing is completed. Avoid putting on the icing too thickly and allow each surface to dry thoroughly in a warm room for 2–3 days – an airing cupboard is useful for the first 2–3 hours. At least three or four coats of icing will be necessary, but the finished thickness must not be more than ¼ inch (½ cm.). Use sandpaper between each coat to remove any roughness.

In between coats, the icing can be kept under a damp cloth, or in an airtight container until it is used again, although before beating, the icing must be transferred from the container to a porcelain bowl. Make up the icing using albumen substitute (or 3 egg whites) and 1 lb. (450 g.) icing sugar, and beating in the left-over icing when the new icing is ready; always use one's judgment for correct stiffness. 3–4 lb. (1½–2 kg.) icing sugar should be sufficient to complete a three-tiered wedding cake, although this inevitably depends on the thickness of the covering and the number of coats needed for a good result. The final coat should be very thin, just enough to give a good finish to the sandpapered surface. The surface must be quite dry before beginning any piping design.

Stiffen any left-over icing by beating well, only adding more sugar or albumen to bring it up to piping strength for working the design. The boards on which the wedding cakes stand must always be whitened with a thin coat of icing and decorated with braiding, trellis or lace work.

Suitable designs for a wedding cake

For general ideas, refer to the pictures on pages 50, 51, 54, 142 and 143, and to pages 50 and 54 for template designs. Ornaments can be bought for the top of a wedding cake – silver vases with natural flowers to match the bride's bouquet, or perhaps a modelled sugar ornament. A useful idea is to buy an inexpensive stiff metal bracelet, or to bend a piece of wire into a similar round shape, and cover it neatly with silver foil. Using stiff icing, attach silver leaves, bought lily-of-the-valley and piped sugar roses to the silver circle, and place it upright on the top of the cake on a pastillage plaque, fixed in position with a star of icing. Prop with tissue paper until dry.

Round or square pillars can be bought from 2–4 inches (5–10 cm.) high. The middle 3-inch (7½-cm.) size is usually the best. If the cake is large, it is advisable to cover the bottom tier with a thin silver board to take the weight of the two tiers above. If the icing is sufficiently dry, this should not be necessary in a two-tier cake.

The stand

Arrangements for hiring a cake stand should be made well in advance of the wedding date. Contact a local confectioner, who will usually be able to hire out a good cake knife as well, and perhaps even a silver vase.

To cut the cake

When the cake has been ceremonially cut by the bride and bridegroom, it should be taken from the reception room to complete the cutting. Begin by cutting straight across the centre, and then into strips 1 inch (2½ cm.) wide across the cake. Lay these pieces flat on a board and cut into fingers. Some icing will always fall away from the cake as it is cut, but this method is far more satisfactory than trying to cut wedge-shaped pieces, which always causes the icing to crumble at the centre of the cake.

Place any loose icing neatly on top of the cake pieces, and arrange on plates to be handed round, or in boxes to be sent away.

A three-tier wedding cake. The nursing and college badges illustrate the careers of the bride and groom.

A three-tier wedding cake ready to be assembled. Square pillars should be used for a square cake.

To design a cake to match the dress

An attractive, personal wedding cake can be made by incorporating the actual lace used for the wedding dress or veil of the bride into the design of the cake. Keep a few scraps of the material, particularly lace edging, and carefully cut out medallions and butterflies, cutting each wing separately. Cut some half medallion shapes for the base of the cake, and place all the lace pieces on waxed paper. Pipe around the edges, and perhaps into the pattern as well. Pipe the centre of the butterfly wings, and leave to dry thoroughly.

Meanwhile, arrange silver braid around the cake in two places, dividing the depth of the cake into thirds. Just overlap the silver braids with a satin ribbon right around the centre of the cake. Pipe stars around the top edge and make hanging loops suspended from them. When these are quite dry, turn the cake upside down and make corresponding loops from the base of the cake. When the loops are dry return the cake to the correct position.

A wedding cake designed to match the lace of the bride's wedding dress.

Make the trellis work for the corners around a wooden spoon handle, or anything else suitably shaped, greased and covered with double waxed paper. Pipe rings for the centrepieces, and strengthen them with fine wire. When these are dry, decorate with small piped roses and leaves – pale pink and green leaves for a birthday cake, but all white for a wedding cake.

When all the preparation is complete, begin to assemble the cake. Fix the trellis pieces in position with piped shells of royal icing. Place the half medallions on the board, and the full medallions correspondingly around the top of the cake, slightly jutting over the edge. Make a body for the butterflies either straight on to the cake, or, previously, on waxed paper; stick the wings into the wet icing and prop them with tissue paper until firm. If the

An American-style wedding cake.

entire butterfly is made first on to waxed paper, fix it to the cake with a small dab of icing.

Lastly, arrange the rings or roses, securing them with a dab of icing on the side nearest the outside of the cake, and prop them up on the inside with tissue paper until dry. If the cake is to be a two-tier wedding cake, complete a similar cake in a smaller size, and place the pillars to hold the second cake inside the rose rings.

An American wedding cake

An American wedding cake is more usually made from a Madeira-type mixture rather than a rich fruit cake mixture. There are several tiers, sometimes with pillars between the tiers and sometimes with the cakes placed directly on top of each other – often two or three cakes are placed on top of each other and the fourth tier is placed on four quite tall pillars. Occasionally the top tier of cake may contain fruit, but it is seldom such a dark, rich mixture as the traditional British wedding cake mixture.

Piping decoration is very elaborate and much use is made of bright ornaments – even minute fountains are used as centrepieces. A white butter cream is sometimes used for a covering.

Other special occasion cakes

Almost any design suitable for a wedding cake may be used for a 21st, 25th or 50th anniversary cake. Where possible choose a personal theme in keeping with the occasion and choose the colours carefully.

Look at the designs in the pictures on pages 94, 162, 167 and 174 and from these you will get ideas for whatever type of cake you want to create. Sometimes a section of one cake can be added to an idea shown in another cake to assemble one's own special idea or scheme.

A 50th anniversary celebration cake.

A prize winning 21st birthday cake in Wedgwood style decorated with a circle of dancing ladies.

A Christmas cake decorated with coloured lace work panels, a lace collar, trellis bells and a candle.

A cake covered with blue royal icing and decorated at the corners with run-out snowflakes.

A Wedgwood-type cake decorated with nativity figures, to form a central panel, and raised lace work.

A Christmas cake decorated with a spray of pastillage Christmas roses, and elaborate lettering.

A Christmas cake decorated with a centrepiece design of choir boys.

A cake decorated in a willow pattern. For a special celebration this could be served with willow pattern china.

A special occasion cake decorated with a needlework design. If liked, the pattern may be gilded.

Ideas for advanced work

Edible glitter

This makes an unusual decoration. It can be made and stored in a small wide-necked jar with a screw top and will keep in a dry place for months. Sprinkle lightly on the top of a flat-iced cake or place a small stencil pattern of a cat, rabbit or duck on top of the iced cake and very lightly brush the space in the stencil with water just to moisten the surface and sprinkle in the coloured glitter. Carefully remove the stencil pattern to leave a shiny glittering figure.

Children's names can be made in the same way; naturally care and patience and a little practice is necessary for a good result.

Glitter recipe

IMPERIAL/METRIC

2 tablespoons water
2 oz./50 g. gum arabic
food colouring (optional)

Oven temperature: cool
(275°F., 140°C., Gas Mark 1)

Put water in a basin, sprinkle in the gum arabic and stand the basin in a pan of warm water (or use a double saucepan). Heat gently and stir until dissolved. Strain the mixture through a muslin, then brush it on to a clean baking tray. Put in a cool oven until dry. Scrape off with a knife, then flake between the fingers and store in an airtight jar. The natural coloured glitter, which is creamy white, sprinkled on cotton wool makes an attractive Christmas table decoration.

An alternative method is to strain the dissolved gum through some muslin and spread it thinly, with a stiff brush, on a sheet of clean polished glass. Dry in a warm room or a very cool oven. When dry and set, scrape or brush the glitter off the glass and crush it into small granules. If liked, add food colouring (light brown and yellow gives a gold effect) to the dissolved gum arabic before straining it and brushing it on to the glass. Store in a small airtight jar.

Rock sugar

IMPERIAL/METRIC

2 lb./900 g. lump or granulated
 sugar
scant ½ pint/3 dl. water
2 oz./50 g. royal icing

Rock sugar can be used as a cake decoration and looks attractive on a Christmas cake to represent snow. (See the picture on page 95.) It is not difficult to make, but the sugar syrup must be removed from the heat at the right moment to prevent discolouration. Also, once the sugar has dissolved it must be boiled quickly to prevent discolouration. It is advisable to make the quantity given opposite, but 1 lb. (450 g.) sugar may be used with safety – any smaller amounts than that are not recommended.

Place the sugar and water in a large saucepan (a copper one is preferable) and put over a low heat until the sugar has dissolved. Increase the heat and boil the mixture rapidly until it reaches 280°F. (138°C.), brushing the insides of the pan with a brush dipped in water from time to time. Remove from the heat and beat in the royal icing (made with egg white, not a substitute) – take care as the mixture rises in the pan. As soon as the mixture settles turn it on to a sheet of greaseproof paper and when cold, break it up and store in an airtight jar.

Rock sugar of various colours may be made by adding a suitable food colouring to the royal icing. Use pieces of green rock sugar to represent trees and bushes.

Icing by numbers

This is a new technique similar to painting by numbers. The design of a stained glass window given on page 189 is an ideal one. Simply cover the pattern with waxed paper and outline the pattern with black, grey or white icing and leave to dry. Then fill in all the spaces numbered one with purple, number two with blue, number three with brown. All the purple must be filled in first and allowed to dry before the blue is put into the number two sections. If not allowed to dry the colours will run into each other. Finally paint in the face and necessary detail with food colouring and an artist's brush. This pattern can be worked directly on to the dry icing on the cake surface by taking a tracing of the picture on greaseproof paper. Use a soft pencil to outline the design on the wrong side, then trace the design directly on to the cake. A feint line will show on the cake and the design can be traced in icing using a No. 1 tube. When dry, these sections can be filled in with run-in icing as described above. Finish the features of the face and details of the dress etc. with food colouring and an artist's fine brush, or an architect's pen which is used for fine drawings: this can be filled with food colouring and used to draw in the features on the icing. This pen gives a better result than a brush and is excellent for fine work on dry icing, if doing advanced work. The line is constantly the same thickness and control of the line is certain. The advanced student will be able to work out further designs with this idea.

If the cake is the same size as the design of the stained glass window when dry, the piece of icing can be removed from the waxed paper and placed on the prepared cake.

Alternatively, the pattern given for the window can be enlarged by adding more sections of colour in the same way. The extra sections should be put on the paper design before beginning the icing.

A stained glass window pattern which would be suitable for working an icing by numbers design. A larger pattern with the colour coding is shown on page 189.

Panel cakes

This idea has a fascination about it; in the cakes in the pictures on pages 90, 162, 166 and 167, the cakes appear six-sided. The six sides are made separately on waxed paper and then placed against the sides of a round cake. The centre picture or spray of flowers is made on the sides of the cake and then framed by the panel.

Bootees and cradle made in royal icing – decorations suitable for the top of a christening cake.

A christening cake for Paul decorated with lace work at the corners.

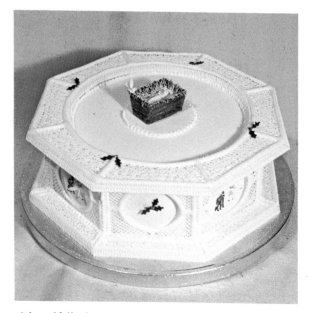

A beautifully decorated cake with trellis work raised panels showing holly and Christmas scenes. The cake has a double lace work collar.

An elaborate cake decorated with a double lace work collar and raised side panels with painted Christmas scenes.

A beautiful eight-sided panel cake with a double collar of open work lace and curtain work.

A special celebration cake decorated with a run-out collar with trellis lace panels on the sides. The wheelbarrow is made from pastillage and filled with piped royal icing roses.

An elaborate panel cake.

A top collar gives a perfect finish by neatening the edges and spaces left by the panel. These panels of lace can be made beforehand and stored in an airtight tin on cotton wool until required, so that it is easy and quick to put this type of cake together; it is advisable to make two or three spares pieces in case of breakage. A tracing pattern for one of these panels is given on page 189. Use your imagination for other patterns for panels.

The same idea can be carried out with eight, 10 or 12 panels, with flowers or scenery depicting the life story of the recipient for the cake. For example, the seven ages of man is an idea which could be taken up for a 50th anniversary cake. Or events in one's own life or scenes from one's garden may be depicted. Another idea is to show the 12 days of Christmas, or scenes of a favourite story. (See the pictures on pages 90, 162, 166 and 167 for panel shapes.)

To complete the panels Fasten the panel design down on glass and cover with waxed paper. Outline the part which is to be lace work with full strength royal icing then complete the lace pattern in royal icing. Outline any remaining lines and fill in the run-in sugar space around the outside and around the centre opening.

Leave all the panels undisturbed until quite dry. Meanwhile, decide on the collar which should not have too much open lace otherwise the open space between the cake and the edge of the panel will show. As an alternative from the collar, corner pieces with fine close lace work and insets of flowers may be used.

To complete the panel cake Measure the cake around the sides and divide into the number of panels made. Arrange a number of sprays of flowers to match the number of panels, or paint scenes on the cake using the original paper pattern to make sure that the flower spray or scene will fit in the opening in the panel. When the number of pictures is complete, very carefully place one panel against the cake with the picture central. With full strength royal icing put a bulb of icing behind the edges of the panel to hold it in place standing up against the side of the cake. Similarly fix the rest of the panels. When all the panels are firmly set, remove the collar from the waxed paper and put a little bulb of royal icing on the top of the cake around the edge. Place the collar in position, or if using lacy sections these should be put on the cake last using the same number of sections as panels. Neaten any space left between the panels with a criss-cross line of royal icing (like lacing a shoe), or straight lines like a ladder.

More elaborate panel cakes

The panel cakes shown on pages 90, 162, 166 and 167 can be made more elaborate by making the sides of the panel larger, or smaller with the correct sized cake inside to fit.

Place several cakes of graduated size on top of one another as a tiered cake – the panels may also be deeper. These of course are exhibition or special occasion cakes as they entail more work.

Needlework patterns on cakes

Some very attractive patterns can be found amongst needlework transfer patterns as well as in books containing patterns for knitting and crochet work.

Sometimes the design is best done on waxed paper and then transferred to the surface on the cake. Others necessitate the work being done directly on to the cake surface. These patterns give a very dainty look and for a special occasion, it may be possible to make a copy of the embroidery of the cloth in use when the cake is being served – see the top two pictures on page 170. The top left picture has elaborate curtain work on the sides and the top edge is decorated with lace motifs. These must be worked on waxed paper and when dry stored until required. Needless to say, extra pieces should be made in case of breakages.

Another delightful special occasion idea is to copy the design on the china used at the tea table. Sprays of flowers are often suitable or the willow pattern as shown in the picture on page 163.

Snowflake patterns

An attractive lacy pattern can be made by copying snowflakes as a design. A few are given opposite. The procedure is the same as for lace work. Put the drawing on glass and cover with waxed paper fastened down with a dot of icing. When dry, remove very carefully and store on cotton wool until required.

Have the cake finished with a good surface in white or a colour. Arrange the snowflake standing up; a dot of icing should secure it. Support on both sides with crushed up tissue paper until firm. Avoid putting too many snowflakes in place at once – allow time for each one to dry.

Some snowflake designs which make attractive lacy pieces for decorating special occasion cakes.

Lace sections for the edge of a cake

These sections are often quite small so there is no weight to be carried by the icing therefore quite open work can be used. (See the drawing opposite and the picture on page 91.)

To make decorations for the heart-shaped cake
Illustrated on page 94
This cake is suitable for an engagement or wedding anniversary. The small half circle lace sections should be made first using any lace pattern wished (a simple pattern of hanging loops has been used with this cake) on waxed paper and left to dry for several

The type of lace pattern which is suitable for use as a lace section for the edge or top of a cake.

A needlework design with lace motifs and green curtain work.

An attractive needlework pattern and a lace trellis inset collar for a special occasion cake.

A Christmas cake decorated with four cushions, bells and a centrepiece of candles and poinsettia.

The perfect surface on this cake shows up the attractive bells decorated with tiny pictures.

Curtain work is shown at its best on this cake, decorated with flowers and holly.

Making lace heart-shaped decorations.

days. About 28 are required for this cake but some extras should be made in case of breakage. Twelve small half-circles for the top of the cake and six slightly smaller half-circles have also to be made to neaten the point of the heart. Also pipe 28 pink sugar roses with royal icing using a small petal tube. Keep these in a box on cotton wool for a few days before using them. Pipe a few extra roses in a slightly deeper colour for decorating the centre of the heart and the sides of the cake. Prepare one or two birds with blue royal icing and a few blue forget-me-not flowers at the same time.

To assemble the heart-shaped cake

Cover a rich fruit cake with a thick coating of almond paste and then a coating of sugar paste (or plastic icing as it is sometimes called). The two together give a very nice flavour. Place the iced cake on the board and complete the decoration around the base of the cake first using 14 of the lace half-circles; place them first before fixing any with icing and when arranged a few dots of icing on the board will be sufficient to hold the work in place. If liked a small pale green leaf may be placed on each side of the pink rose; place the rose in position when the leaves are made on the cake board. At the same time complete the sides of the cake with a simple piped bow and a spray of flowers as shown in the picture.

The centre of the cake can be completed next. Have ready a run-out dry heart or place a cardboard template in position and outline around the template and run in the soft icing. Prick out any bubbles and leave to dry. When dry write in the names and arrange the spray of flowers and the blue bird holding a gold ring. The ring can be made from a roll of pastillage and gilded with gold powder mixed with a drop of gin, or use a bought metal ring. Next, pipe a row of stars around the centre heart shape and while still wet fix in the 12 small lace half-circles. Also pipe a row of stars down the edge of the heart and fix the six half-circles as shown in the picture. A row of stars may be put around the base of the cake to neaten the space between the cake and the half-circles if required.

Next, put a guide line around the top edge of the cake with a pencil and measure with a strip of paper to help when making the curtain work lines which are worked from the inside outwards. With a No. 5 star tube, pipe three rows of icing rope around the edge of the cake as in the 3-D work. Allow the first row to dry a little before putting on the second row and again after placing the last row. When this raised wall is quite dry pipe stars on the top edge to hold the remaining half-circles. It is advisable to plan these before starting and then place the first two each side the point and the next two at the centre back placing the others in between. Only make sufficient stars at a time to hold the half circles in case they become too dry.

A 21st birthday cake decorated with curtain work.

Finally, and with special care, pipe in the pink lines of curtain work. Starting from the inside to the outside on the raised wall. Care must be taken not to break the half-circles when leaning over the work. A low table is easiest. Now put in the sugar roses and leaves, if used, between the half-circles. Neaten the curtain work with a line and a row of dots on the inner edge.

To make moulds

Knowing how to make moulds is a useful accomplishment. This method enables one to take an imprint of a raised patterned surface and then produce a mould in which repeats of the raised pattern can be made for decorating a cake surface. The most useful for cake decorating are the white figures seen on Wedgwood vases for reproduction for decoration on the Wedgwood cakes. (See the pictures on pages 99 and 102.)

To make a mould for Wedgwood work

a Wedgwood vase, or plastic
    imitation
small pieces of wood about 2
    inches (5 cm.) by 2½ inches
    (6 cm.)
1 lb. (450 g.) dental plaster or
    plaster of Paris (the dental
    plaster is a finer quality and
    makes a better mould)
water

Having decided on the Wedgwood figure to be reproduced and prepared several pieces of smooth wood, put about 4 tablespoons plaster in a basin. Add enough water to make a thick creamy paste which will not run but will spread like soft butter. Spread the plaster thickly, about ½ inch (1 cm.) deep, over one of the figures on the vase making the surface as neat as possible. Quickly spread a similar round of plaster ¼ inch (½ cm.) on a piece of wood and press the wood and plaster on to the plaster on the figure on the vase carefully like a sandwich. Prop up with crushed tissue paper on a table to prevent the vase from moving and leave overnight to dry.

Next day, carefully pull off the plaster mould using the piece of wood as a handle. If a real Wedgwood vase is used great care must be taken to avoid breaking the vase – it is really safer to use an imitation one. Repeat the process with another figure.

Moulds can be made of all kinds of raised patterned figures in this way – patterns on plant pots or raised patterns on wall plaques. Use one's own judgement on the quantity of plaster to use according to the size of the figure. When the mould is completed any plaster left in the basin can be removed by soaking it in cold water. If any plaster adheres to the vase, soaking in cold water will remove it. If there is any difficulty in removing the plaster mould from the vase soak it in cold water and try again. A good tip is to brush the surface with a fine brush and a little olive oil as some surfaces are not as easy to remove the mould from as others. Again, this is a job that needs experience and will become easier with practice.

If air bubbles have appeared in the mould shake the plaster in the basin before using it next time.

A 21st birthday cake decorated with run-out figures for a golfing enthusiast.

A neatly decorated cake with a square run-out collar and a painted centrepiece.

A 50th wedding anniversary cake decorated in white and gold.

A mirror used to represent a lake for icing swans (see page 141). The swans may be filled with small sweets, piped flowers or fresh fruit. The lilies are made from pastillage.

To make the pastillage figures using the moulds

2 tablespoons normal strength
   royal icing
½ teaspoon gum tragacanth
icing sugar, sifted

Mix the royal icing and gum tragacanth together and beat well. Allow to stand for 5–6 hours, or overnight if wished, covered with a wet cloth (or use an airtight plastic container). When ready, add enough sifted icing sugar to make a firm paste. Knead well until smooth and white; keep covered when not in use.

Press out a little of the prepared paste between the thumb and fingers to form an oval shape about ⅛ inch (¼ cm.) thick and large enough to fill the mould. Press the oval into the mould of the Wedgwood figure and smooth off with a palette knife so it is level with the plaster mould edge of the figure. Continue filling the other moulds made and after about 3–5 minutes the first figure in the mould should be set enough to remove. Use a pin to remove the pastillage figure from the mould. Place on a flat surface of waxed paper and tidy the edges with the pin and leave to become quite dry. This is for a flat figure but if required for a round cake place the figure on the round cake tin with a piece of waxed paper under the figure until dry. This gives a slightly curved figure which will fit the round cake better. With the pin, tidy the edges of the figure, e.g. around the edge of the arms, etc., until the work is completed. When dry, store all the figures on waxed paper in an airtight tin until required. If any difficulty is experienced in removing the casts try dusting the moulds lightly with cornflour.

To fix the Wedgwood figures on the cake

When the cake has been coated with three coats or layers of lighter Wedgwood blue icing and a good surface made, complete any edging depending on the design of the cake and finally place a little normal strength royal icing on the back of the figure and place in position carefully.

To make the standing figures shown in the picture on page 162, they must be iced by hand. Turn the figure on its face on waxed paper and pipe a fine line of icing, backwards and forwards, and along the figure's arms etc., to make a good copy. Smooth out the plain surfaces with a slightly damp brush, as for piping the figures by hand.

Colour may be added to the pastillage and should be kneaded in well to give an even shade throughout.

Candy clay

IMPERIAL/METRIC

2 tablespoons cold water
½ oz./15 g. gum tragacanth
3 oz./75 g. cornflour, sifted
4 oz./100 g. icing sugar, sifted
flavourings and food colouring

This is a very hard-drying medium for modelling or moulding cake decorations such as ornaments, flowers or models (such as the gondola or wheelbarrow) which require strength. It is more for display and decoration, but is edible and is often eaten and enjoyed by children, or those who like hard sweetmeats. It is similar to pastillage but much stronger.

Place the water in a plastic bowl with a lid. Sift the tragacanth, cornflour and sugar together on to paper and then sift again into

176

the water, gently beating with a fork until mixed. Put on the lid to make airtight and leave overnight. Dust clean washed hands lightly with cornflour and knead the mixture until it is smooth and white; add the flavouring and colouring as required.

Roll it out on a board or sheet of glass dusted with cornflour and place the paper pattern of the model to be made on top and cut around it with a knife. Dry the pieces of the model on the glass and when they are firm and dry use to build the model. Royal icing can be used to secure the pieces together. Gather up any trimmings and keep them in the airtight bowl in the refrigerator until required again. Open the bowl and re-knead from time to time. Colour may be kneaded into the candy clay for making flowers etc. The surface can also be painted when making flowers with various markings, such as spots and lines for lilies and orchids. Prop up the petals with crushed tissue paper until set and firm. When moulding flowers, the hands can be slightly greased with lard but rubbed dry again with a cloth; the slightly greasy surface softens the hands to make moulding this dry paste a little easier. Finally, some peppermint oil can be kneaded into the trimmings. Roll out and cut into tiny rounds with a cutter and use as hard peppermints.

Sugar Easter eggs

IMPERIAL/METRIC

1 pair Easter egg moulds
2 oz./50 g. flavoured pastillage
cornflour
sugar flowers
royal icing

Rub the inside of the egg mould with a clean dry cloth to polish it and remove any finger marks. Dust evenly with cornflour. Roll out half the pastillage and press carefully into the egg mould making a neat, even covering and leaving no cracks. Keep the second half under cover while the first half is being used. Repeat the process with the second half and trim the edges evenly. Leave overnight to dry. Next day, carefully remove the two halves and secure together with royal icing. Decorate the join with stars or scrolls. When quite firm and dry, arrange a spray of sugar flowers and if liked pipe a child's name. Place in the centre of a square of cellophane and gather up the edges to enclose the egg and tie with ribbon.

To make a sugar lace doily design

Lace decorations may be taken from a paper lace doily. Place the doily on a flat surface and cover with waxed paper. Fasten down carefully outside the pattern with a dot of icing. Using a No. 1 tube and white or coloured icing proceed to outline the design of the doily carefully making neat points in the pattern and leaving no unevenness. Run-in soft sugar for any solid parts of the doily. When dry over-pipe any necessary parts and strengthen the edge with an extra row of piping.

Cover a cake neatly with delicately-coloured sugar paste. Tie a ribbon around the cake and place on a large silver thick board.

Carefully remove the perfectly dry icing lace from the paper doily by placing it to the edge of an upturned tray and peel off the waxed paper by gently pulling it downwards and turning the icing doily round so that a little is removed at a time. When the surface is quite loose carefully lift the lace sugar doily to the top of the cake on the wax paper and slide the wax paper away. Should the icing crack or break it can be repaired but it will be necessary to wait for a day or two until it is quite dry.

Two cakes decorated with sugar lace tops. The patterns have been taken from paper doilies.

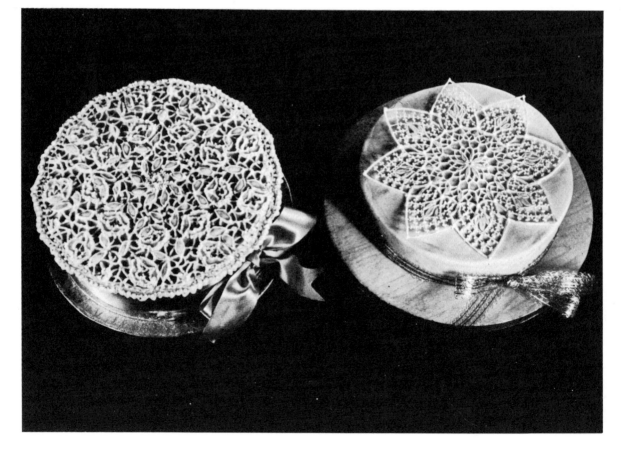

Recipes

Victoria sandwich cake

IMPERIAL/METRIC

4 oz./110 g. margarine or butter
4 oz./110 g. castor sugar
2 large eggs
4 oz./110 g. self-raising flour (or plain flour and 1 teaspoon baking powder)

Oven temperature: moderate (350°F., 180°C., Gas Mark 4)
Cooking time: 15–20 minutes (for the two cakes) or 35 minutes (for the one cake)
Makes: two 7-inch (18-cm.) cakes, or one 8-inch (20-cm.)

Grease two 7-inch (18-cm.) sandwich cake tins, or one 8-inch (20-cm.) tin and line the base with a round of greaseproof paper. To give a better result, place the eggs (in their shells) in a cup of warm water at room temperature for 5 minutes.

Cream the margarine and sugar until very light. Add one egg and 1 teaspoon flour and beat well. Add the second egg and another teaspoon of flour and continue beating. Sift in the remaining flour, and fold in lightly. Smooth into the prepared tins (or tin) and bake in a moderate oven for 15–20 minutes, or for 35 minutes for the larger cake. When cooked, turn out and cool on a wire rack. Store in a tin until needed.

Decorate with glacé icing, butter cream, or fudge or caramel icing.

Madeira cake
Follow the recipe for a Victoria sandwich cake, but use 6 oz. (175 g.) flour. Bake the mixture in a deep 8-inch (20-cm.) cake tin. Decorate with glacé icing or butter cream, fudge or caramel icing

To adapt the recipe for a crinoline lady cake, bake the mixture in a greased ovenproof basin for $1\frac{1}{4}$ hours.

Chocolate cake

IMPERIAL/METRIC

8 oz./225 g. self-raising flour (or plain flour and 1 teaspoon baking powder)
2 oz./50 g. cocoa powder
4 oz./100 g. lard
7 oz./200 g. castor sugar
1 egg
$\frac{1}{4}$ pint/1$\frac{1}{2}$ dl. milk
$\frac{1}{2}$ teaspoon vanilla essence

Oven temperature: moderate (350°F., 180°C., Gas Mark 4) for the buns, or 325°F., 170°C., Gas Mark 3 for the cake
Cooking time: about 12 minutes or $1\frac{1}{4}$ hours
Makes about 25 buns or one 8-inch (20-cm.) cake

Sift the flour (and baking powder, if used) and cocoa powder twice. Rub in the lard. Add the sugar and stir in beaten egg and milk to a soft mixture. Add the vanilla essence. Put teaspoonfuls into round-based greased bun tins and bake in a moderate oven for about 12 minutes, or bake in a prepared 8-inch (20-cm.) cake tin at the lower temperature for about $1\frac{1}{4}$ hours. Cool on a wire rack.

This mixture may also be used for a sandwich cake, chocolate mushrooms or chocolate butterfly cakes, or as a base for the Italian chocolate torton or a large mushroom cake.

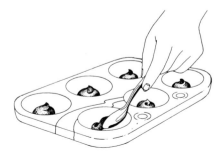

Plain white cake

IMPERIAL/METRIC

8 oz./225 g. self-raising flour (or
    plain flour and 1 teaspoon
    baking powder)
4 oz./110 g. margarine
½ oz./15 g. lard
4 oz./110 g. castor sugar
2 eggs (or 1 egg and a little
    milk)
vanilla essence

Oven temperature: moderate
(350°F., 180°C., Gas Mark 4)
Cooking time: 1 hour–1 hour
10 minutes
Makes: one 7-inch (18-cm.) cake

Sift the flour (and baking powder, if used) into a basin. Rub in the margarine and lard. Add the sugar. Whisk the eggs (or egg and milk) until frothy, and stir into the flour etc., beating lightly. Turn into a 7-inch (18-cm.) prepared cake tin and bake in a moderate oven for 1 hour–1 hour 10 minutes. Cool on a wire rack.

This cake is suitable for cutting into layers and filling. To vary the layers, use alternately with chocolate cake, or a cake coloured pink with food colouring or a raspberry blancmange powder mixed with the flour.

VARIATIONS

Plain fruit cake Add 4–6 oz. (100–175 g.) currants or sultanas with the sugar.

Russian sandwich Divide the mixture into three. Colour one-third pink and flavour one-third with cocoa powder. Put spoonfuls of the plain mixture into a greased 2-lb. (1-kg.) loaf tin, leaving spaces between the spoonfuls. Brush over with apricot jam. Put spoonfuls of the pink mixture into half the spaces. Add a little milk to the cocoa-flavoured mixture and use to fill in the remaining spaces. Carefully hollow the centre of the mixture to make the cake rise evenly, but avoid mixing the colours unless a marbled effect is required. Bake in a moderate oven for 1 hour–1 hour 10 minutes. Cool on a wire rack.

Light fruit cake

IMPERIAL/METRIC

4 oz./110 g. margarine or butter
4 oz./110 g. castor sugar
2 eggs
6 oz./175 g. self-raising flour (or
    plain flour and ½ teaspoon
    baking powder)
4–6 oz./100–175 g. currants,
    sultanas or chopped raisins or
    4 oz./100 g. glacé cherries
    or 2 oz./50 g. chopped walnuts
    or a mixture of nuts, cherries
    and sultanas
½ oz./15 g. ground almonds
    (optional)

Oven temperature: moderate
(350°F., 180°C., Gas Mark 4)
Cooking time: about 1 hour
Makes: one 1-lb. (½-kg.) loaf
cake, one 7-inch (18-cm.)
round cake

Cream the margarine and sugar until light and fluffy. Add 1 egg and 1 teaspoon flour. Beat well, and add the second egg and another teaspoon flour. Continue beating until light, but do not allow the mixture to curdle. Fold in the remaining sifted flour, together with the rest of the ingredients

Turn into the greased loaf tin or cake tin. Slightly hollow out the centre of the mixture and bake in a moderate oven for about 1 hour, until firm to the touch. Cool on a wire rack.

Before baking a light fruit cake mixture, slightly hollow out the centre so that the baked cake has a flat surface.

Canadian fruit cake

IMPERIAL/METRIC

5 oz./150 g. butter or margarine
4½ oz./115 g. castor sugar
2 large eggs
7 oz./200 g. self-raising flour and
    ¼ teaspoon baking powder (or
    plain flour and 1 heaped
    teaspoon baking powder)
1 16-oz./450-g. can chopped
    pineapple, well drained
9 oz./250 g. sultanas, chopped
3 oz./75 g. chopped candied peel
2 tablespoons brandy or sherry

Oven temperature: moderate
(325°F., 170°C., Gas Mark 3)
Cooking time: 1–1½ hours
Makes: one 8-inch (20-cm.) cake

Cream the margarine and sugar until light and fluffy. Add the eggs one at a time, with a teaspoon of flour, beating after each addition. Fold in the sifted flour and baking powder; fold in the fruit, and lastly, the brandy or sherry.

Turn into a prepared 8-inch (20-cm.) cake tin and bake in a moderate oven for 1–1½ hours. Cool on a wire rack.

Cover lightly with almond or sugar paste, or both.

Christmas or birthday cake

IMPERIAL/METRIC

8 oz./225 g. margarine or butter
8 oz./225 g. dark brown sugar
4 eggs
12 oz./350 g. plain flour
1 teaspoon mixed spice
1 tablespoon black treacle
grated rind of 1 orange
grated rind of 1 lemon
2 lb./1 kg. mixed fruit
2 oz./50 g. glacé cherries
1 oz./25 g. ground almonds
2 oz./50 g. candied peel
little milk if necessary

Oven temperature: cool
(275°F., 140°C., Gas Mark 1)
Cooking time: 4–5 hours
Makes: one 8-inch (20-cm.)
cake

Line an 8-inch (20-cm.) cake tin with greaseproof paper and tie some brown paper around the outside of the tin. If possible, clean and dry the fruit the previous day.

Cream the fat and sugar, add the eggs one at a time with a teaspoon of the flour. Beat after adding each egg. Beat in the spice, treacle and grated orange and lemon rinds and the sifted flour. Add the fruit, cherries, almonds, peel, and, if necessary for a fairly soft consistency, a little milk.

Turn into the prepared tin and bake in the centre of a cool oven for 4–5 hours. The long, slow cooking gives the cake a good, rich, dark colour – avoid opening the oven door while the cake is cooking.

For a richer Christmas or birthday cake, use the wedding cake recipe on page 158.

Sponge cake

IMPERIAL/METRIC

3 oz./75 g. plain flour
2 large eggs
2 oz./50 g. castor sugar
1 tablespoon milk
vanilla essence (optional)

Oven temperature: moderately hot (375°F., 190°C., Gas Mark 5)
Cooking time: 15–20 minutes
Makes: two 6-inch (15-cm.) cakes

Sift the flour, and follow the method for making a sponge roll. Have ready two 6-inch (15-cm.) sandwich cake tins, greased and dredged with flour and sugar. Divide the mixture equally between the two tins. Bake in the centre of a moderately hot oven (if possible, bake the two cakes on the same shelf) for 15–20 minutes. Cool on a wire rack with a cloth underneath, to prevent the rack marking the cakes.

Sandwich the cakes together using any of the fillings given on pages 24–32.

If preferred, the mixture may be baked in one 8-inch (20-cm.) tin for 25–30 minutes, and when cold split in half and filled.

Genoese sandwich and small fancy cakes

IMPERIAL/METRIC

2½ oz./60 g. flour and ½ oz./15 g. cornflour (or use 3 oz./75 g. flour)
3 large eggs
4 oz./100 g. castor sugar
3 oz./75 g. butter

Oven temperature: moderately hot (400°F., 200°C., Gas Mark 6)
Cooking time: 20 minutes
Makes: two 7-inch (18-cm.) cakes

Slightly warm and sift the flour and cornflour twice on to a plate or paper. Whisk the eggs and sugar over hot water until thick and creamy (sufficiently long to trap enough air to eliminate the need for baking powder). This will take about 20 minutes – less if you are using an electric mixer. When the mixture is thick and creamy, fold in the melted butter, and then the flour, lightly but thoroughly. Turn the mixture into two prepared 7-inch (18-cm.) sandwich tins and bake in a moderately hot oven for about 20 minutes. Cool on a wire rack.

This mixture may also be baked in a Swiss roll tin, and when cold cut into small pieces to make petits fours, domino cakes, or other small fancy cakes. These will keep well, and the mixture is firmer than a sponge cake, and is not so liable to crumble.

Sponge or alpine roll

IMPERIAL/METRIC

2 large eggs
2 oz./50 g. castor sugar
2 oz./50 g. plain flour
1 tablespoon milk
2 tablespoons jam

Oven temperature: moderately hot (400°F., 200°C., Gas Mark 6)
Cooking time: 7 minutes
Makes: one roll

Put the eggs and sugar in a basin placed over a bowl of hot water. Whisk for about 20 minutes, until thick and creamy. (If the whisking is done with an electric mixer it will take less time.) When nearly ready, remove from the hot water and continue whisking to cool the mixture. Sift the flour and fold in lightly. Fold in the milk. Pour the mixture into a greased and floured Swiss roll tin and spread evenly. Bake in the centre of a moderately hot oven for 7 minutes.

While the cake is baking, heat the jam and spread a sheet of greaseproof paper on the table. Dredge the paper well with castor sugar. When the cake is ready, turn out carefully on to the paper, and quickly trim off ¼ inch (½ cm.) all around the edges. Spread with the warm jam and roll up quickly. Hold in position for a few minutes until quite firm and then leave to cool on a wire rack, covered with paper or a cloth.

To fill the roll with cream instead of jam, roll up the roll without any filling, and when cold, carefully unroll and fill with lightly whipped cream.

Self-raising flour, or plain flour and baking powder, may be used if preferred, but if sufficiently beaten, the mixture should have enough air incorporated to produce a well risen cake without the addition of baking powder.

To make a chocolate roll (suitable for making a chocolate log or Dougal cake), use 1½ oz. (40 g.) flour and 1 oz. (25 g.) cocoa powder.

Mushroom cake

IMPERIAL/METRIC

4 oz./110 g. butter or margarine
4 oz./110 g. castor sugar
2 eggs
6 oz./175 g. self-raising flour
1 oz./25 g. cocoa powder
2 tablespoons milk
few drops vanilla essence
filling (see method)
chocolate topping (see page 16)
meringue mushrooms (see below)

Oven temperature: moderate (350°F., 180°C., Gas Mark 4)
Cooking time: 40–50 minutes.
Makes: one 7- or 8-inch (18- or 20-cm.) cake

Cream the butter and sugar together. Add the eggs, one at a time, with 1 tablespoon of the flour. Sift the remaining flour with the cocoa powder and sift a second time, into the mixture. Fold together lightly and add the milk and vanilla essence. Turn into a 7- or 8-inch (18- or 20-cm.) cake tin lined with greaseproof paper. Bake in the centre of a moderate oven for 40–50 minutes. Cool on a wire rack.

When cool, cut the cake through the centre and sandwich together with a filling (see pages 24–32). Coat the top with chocolate topping and decorate with meringue mushrooms.

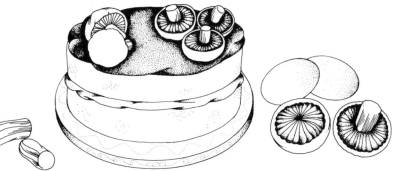

Meringue mushrooms

IMPERIAL/METRIC

3 egg whites
6 oz./175 g. castor sugar
few drops lemon juice
½ teaspoon vanilla essence

Oven temperature: very cool (225°F., 110°C., Gas Mark ¼)
Cooking time: about 3 hours
Makes: 20

Whisk the egg whites very stiffly. Fold in the sugar, lemon juice and vanilla essence. Spoon the mixture into a large forcing bag with a ½- to ¾-inch (1- to 1½-cm.) nozzle and pipe rounds without points, for mushroom heads, on to a greased and floured baking tray. Pipe out an equal number of 2-inch (5-cm.) lengths for stems. Cook in a very cool oven for about 3 hours, until firm and dry but not browned. When cold, spread the flat side of the heads with chocolate butter cream, or icing, and mark with a fork to represent the mushroom gills; press a stem into each mushroom top. Use to decorate the mushroom cake (see the previous recipe).

Any left-over meringues can be sandwiched together with whipped cream, or stored (without cream) in an airtight tin.

Gâteau Nola

IMPERIAL/METRIC

sauce
8 oz./225 g. plain chocolate
3½ oz./90 g. castor sugar
¼ pint/1½ dl. water
1½ teaspoons instant coffee
   powder
2 teaspoons vanilla essence
pastry
8 oz./200 g. plain flour
2 oz./50 g. cornflour
pinch salt
5 oz./150 g. butter
filling and topping
½ pint/3 dl. double cream
little rum or Cointreau
grated chocolate
piped sugar flowers and leaves

Oven temperature: hot
(425°F., 220°C., Gas Mark 7)
Cooking time: about 8 minutes
for each layer
Serves: 6

Put the chocolate, sugar, water and instant coffee powder into a saucepan and melt together very slowly until the sauce is smooth; stir in the vanilla essence. Divide in half and leave to cool to room temperature.

Sift together the flour, cornflour and salt and rub in the butter. Stir in half of the chocolate sauce and beat the mixture until well blended and smooth. Divide the mixture into six and spread each portion on to the bottom of six inverted 8-inch (20-cm.) tins (or use foil cases); smooth the edges and bake each, separately, in a hot oven for 5–8 minutes. Remove from tins while still hot. Cool on a wire rack.

Whisk the cream until thickened, fold in the remaining chocolate sauce, flavour to taste with rum or Cointreau, and use to sandwich the chocolate layers together, leaving enough to top the gâteau. Sprinkle with grated chocolate. Chill thoroughly before serving. Just before serving decorate with piped sugar flowers and leaves.

Nut torte

IMPERIAL/METRIC

5 oz./150 g. self-raising flour
10 oz./275 g. castor sugar
5 eggs, separated
17 oz./475 g. icing sugar
2 tablespoons coffee powder or
   2 oz./50 g. plain chocolate
vanilla essence (optional)
4 tablespoons rum
6 oz./175 g. butter
2 oz./50 g. almonds, chopped
3 oz./75 g. whole almonds,
   browned

Oven temperature: moderately
hot (375°F., 190°C., Gas Mark
5)
Cooking time: 15 minutes
Serves: 6–8

This recipe comes from Austria.

Sift the flour and castor sugar together four times. Beat the egg whites very stiffly and fold in the flour and sugar mixture. Spread a thin layer in six greased 6-inch (15-cm.) or 7-inch (18-cm.) sandwich tins. (Or use foil dishes.) Cook in a moderately hot oven for 15 minutes. Cool the cakes on a wire rack.

In a double saucepan put the egg yolks, 3 oz. (75 g.) of the icing sugar, the coffee powder or chocolate, essence (if used) and rum. Cook, stirring, over a gentle heat until thickened. Cool. Put the butter and remaining icing sugar in a bowl and cream until light. Add the egg yolk mixture, a little at a time, and beat until thick. Spread the cream mixture on the sponge layers. Sprinkle five layers with the chopped almonds and sandwich the layers together, placing the one without nuts on top. Smooth the top layer of filling, or mark in a pattern with a fork or knife and decorate with the whole browned almonds and if liked, chocolate leaves (see the chocolate icing recipe on page 13).

Pavlova Sybil

IMPERIAL/METRIC

3 egg whites
pinch salt
6 oz./175 g. castor sugar
1 teaspoon cornflour
½ teaspoon vanilla essence
1 teaspoon vinegar
fresh or frozen strawberries
double cream

Oven temperature: cool
(300°F., 150°C., Gas Mark 2)
Cooking time: about 1 hour
Serves: 6

Line an 8- or 9-inch (20- or 23-cm.) sandwich tin with greased paper. Beat the egg whites and salt until very stiff. Beat in half the sugar. Mix the cornflour thoroughly with the rest of the sugar and fold it into the mixture, lightly and carefully, with the essence and vinegar. Spread in the tin and smooth out with a palette knife. Bake in a cool oven for about 1 hour, until firm on the outside and still soft inside.

Turn upside down on to a large dish and leave to cool – the pavlova will shrink slightly. Arrange the fruit on the top and pipe with whipped cream using a large star tube in a double grease-proof icing bag. Alternatively, place teaspoonfuls of whipped cream between the strawberries.

In place of the strawberries any drained, canned fruit may be used.

Gingerbread pastry

IMPERIAL/METRIC

1 lb./450 g. plain flour
½ teaspoon salt
1 tablespoon bicarbonate of soda
½ teaspoon ground cinnamon
2 teaspoons ground ginger
4 oz./100 g. margarine
8 oz./225 g. soft brown sugar
6 oz./175 g. treacle
about 2 tablespoons evaporated
   milk

Oven temperature: moderate
(350°F., 180°C., Gas Mark 4)
Cooking time: 10–15 minutes
Makes: about 60 biscuits,
depending on the size

Sift the flour, salt, bicarbonate of soda, cinnamon and ginger into a bowl. Melt the margarine, sugar and treacle – do not allow to boil. Cool a little and then pour on to the dry ingredients. Mix well and add enough milk to make into a firm pastry. Roll out and cut into shapes. Place on greased baking trays and bake in a moderate oven for 10–15 minutes. Cool on a wire rack.

Alternatively, make a cardboard pattern to cut out pieces for a model house, or draw a figure of an animal. Place on the rolled out pastry and cut around the shape. Bake, cool and decorate.

Shrewsbury biscuits

IMPERIAL/METRIC

2 oz./50 g. margarine
2 oz./50 g. castor sugar
1 small egg yolk
4 oz./100 g. plain flour

Oven temperature: moderately
hot (375°F., 190°C., Gas Mark
5)
Cooking time: about 10 minutes
Makes: about 12

Cream the margarine and sugar until very light. Add a little of the egg yolk and some sifted flour alternately until all the flour has been worked in and a firm dough has been made – all the egg yolk may not be needed. Set the dough aside in a cool place for about 1 hour. Roll out on a floured board and cut into shapes with a cutter. Put on a greased baking tray and bake in a moderately hot oven for about 10 minutes, until pale brown, changing the position of the biscuits on the tray halfway through the cooking time.

Cool on a wire rack until crisp. Store in an airtight tin, and decorate when needed.

Decorated ratafia biscuits

IMPERIAL/METRIC

2 oz./50 g. butter or margarine
8 oz./225 g. castor sugar
8 oz./225 g. ground almonds
3 egg whites
½ teaspoon home-made (see opposite) or bought ratafia essence
royal icing
food colouring

Oven temperature: cool (300°F., 150°C., Gas Mark 2)
Cooking time: 10 minutes
Makes: about 48

Cream the butter until softened. Mix in the sugar and ground almonds. Whisk the egg whites until foamy but not stiff, and add the ratafia essence. Mix all the ingredients together with a wooden spoon. Place rice paper on baking trays and drop teaspoonfuls of the mixture well apart on the rice paper. Bake in a cool oven for 20 minutes, until pale brown. When cool remove from the baking trays and cut or tear the surplus rice paper around each biscuit. Store in an airtight tin. To decorate the biscuits pipe the centre with a star of royal icing using various colours of icing.

Desiccated coconut may be substituted for the ground almonds.

Ratafia essence
This is a very old recipe from Ireland.

Gather hawthorn buds when in bloom in the spring. Fill a ½-pint (3-dl.) bottle three-quarters full with the buds. Heat about ¼ pint (1½ dl.) whiskey in a saucepan. When simmering, remove from the heat and cover until cool. When cold, pour over the blossoms, cork and seal the bottle with sticky tape or melted wax. The essence will be ready for use in about 10 days. Pour off the liquid into another bottle and cork tightly. This will keep for years but must be tightly sealed or it will evaporate.

Sisters' bows

IMPERIAL/METRIC

5 oz./150 g. butter
8 oz./225 g. plain flour
pinch salt
1 tablespoon castor sugar
1 tablespoon ice cold water
½ teaspoon lemon juice
1 egg yolk
fat or oil for deep frying
simple syrup (see below)
few piped sugar flowers

Cooking time: few minutes
Makes: 12

This recipe comes from South Africa.

Make a rich pastry by rubbing the butter into the flour. Add the salt and sugar. Add the ice cold water and the lemon juice to the egg yolk and beat together. Add to the rubbed-in mixture to form a stiff dough. (All the liquid may not be required.) Place the dough in a cool place for 1 hour. Roll out the pastry on a floured board and cut into ½-inch (1-cm.) strips. Tie these strips into bows or knots and leave in a cold place to become quite firm. Meanwhile, heat the fat in a strong pan for deep frying. Place the bows in a wire basket in a single layer and lower gently into the heated fat; cook until pale brown, then drain on absorbent paper. Have ready the simple syrup and while the pastry bows are still hot dip them quickly, one at a time, in the cold syrup. Using a draining spoon, place the biscuits on a large wire rack to drain, with a plate underneath. When cold, decorate each bow with a small coloured flower. Arrange on a doily and serve, or store in an airtight tin.

Simple syrup
Place 1 lb. (450 g.) granulated sugar and 1 pint (6 dl.) water in a saucepan. Place over a low heat to dissolve the sugar, then boil the mixture for 2–3 minutes. Leave to cool. This syrup may be stored in an airtight container and used as required. Strain the syrup before using it for a second time.

Real Scottish shortbread

IMPERIAL/METRIC

12 oz./300 g. plain flour
4 oz./100 g. cornflour
4 oz./100 g. castor sugar
8 oz./200 g. butter

Oven temperature: moderate
(350°F., 180°C., Gas Mark 4)
Cooking time: 30 minutes

Mix the flour, cornflour and sugar together. Rub in the butter and knead well to form a soft dough. Flour a shortbread mould lightly, then press the mixture into the mould.

Turn the shape out on to a baking tray and bake in a moderate oven for 30 minutes. Cool on a wire rack.

If a mould is not available, form the mixture into a ball, then roll it out to $\frac{1}{2}$ inch (1 cm.) thick on a lightly floured board. Prick all over, and pinch around the edges between the thumb and first finger. Place on a baking tray and cook as above.

Place waxed paper over the design shown in the drawing and outline the leaves and base of the flower, with green royal icing. Run in soft icing. When dry outline with green icing using a No. 0 tube. Using purple icing complete the flowers by placing fine lines touching each other over the pattern. Lift carefully when dry and use to decorate the shortbread. Secure the decoration to the shortbread with a little icing.

Lollipop cookies

IMPERIAL/METRIC

4 oz./100 g. butter or margarine
4 oz./100 g. castor sugar
grated rind and juice of $\frac{1}{2}$ lemon
2 egg yolks
8 oz./200 g. plain flour
18 lollipop sticks
royal icing
18 small eating apples

Oven temperature: moderate
(350°F., 180°C., Gas Mark 4)
Cooking time: about 20 minutes
Makes: 18

These are ideal to serve for a children's party.

Cream the butter and sugar and add the grated lemon rind. Beat the egg yolks with the lemon juice. Add half the egg and lemon to the creamed mixture and half the flour; add more egg and flour alternately until all the flour is used and a firm pastry is produced – all the egg and lemon may not be required. Place the mixture in a cool place for 1 hour. Roll out to $\frac{1}{4}$ inch ($\frac{1}{2}$ cm.) thick on a floured board and cut 18 rounds with a 2-inch (5-cm.) cutter. Place on a greased tray for baking. Carefully press a lollipop stick at the side and secure with some of the pastry trimmings. Bake in a moderate oven for 20 minutes, until pale brown. Cool. With royal icing pipe a child's name on each biscuit and make a frilly edge of icing, or pipe a face, or greetings.

Place the apples on a tray and make a hole in the top with a spare lollipop stick. Insert a biscuit in each apple.

A box of strawberries

IMPERIAL/METRIC

1 packet strawberry jelly
1 small can sweetened condensed
    milk
about 1 lb./450 g. desiccated
    coconut
red food colouring (optional)
little raspberry jam
artificial strawberry tops, or
    make stems from almond paste
    coloured green

Dissolve the jelly in one-quarter of the amount of water stated on the packet. Cool and stir into the canned milk. Add enough of the desiccated coconut to make a stiff mixture. Add red food colouring if required. Roll into balls and form into strawberry shapes. Press a strawberry top in each. Brush with raspberry jam to give the effect of strawberry seeds. Place on waxed paper until quite firm and dry. Arrange on a dish or in a strawberry basket.

Tracings and patterns

Other fairytale tableaux can be made in icing by taking patterns from children's story books. When taking patterns from these tracings arrange the figures in proportion to each other.

A panel pattern. Use six panels for the sides of an 8-inch (20-cm.) cake.

1 Purple
2 Blue
3 Brown
4 White
5 Pale blue
6 Lavender
7 Green
8 Pink
9 Pale pink
10 Red
11 Pale green
12 Yellow
13 Peach

To make curved wings, work the wings over a hard-boiled egg or a greased, curved cup.

Index